a Qi Note book

BOOKS BY SU TERRY

♪

INSIDE THE MIND OF A MUSICIAN

I WAS A JAZZ MUSICIAN FOR THE FBI

FOR THE CURIOUS

FOR

the

CURIOUS

Su Terry

Cover photo by James Richard Kao

FOR THE CURIOUS

ISBN 978-0-9988844-0-0

ACKNOWLEDGEMENTS

Many thanks to those individuals whose gifts of books, films, knowledge and experiences contributed to the writing of these essays: Gil Barretto, Dr. Harry Saras, Elizabeth Crefin, William C. Phillips, Julia French, Meredith Miller, Diego & Milagros Palma, Linda Gerkensmeyer, Derwyn Holder; and the New York Times writers whose research alerted me to additional subjects worthy of exploration.

In memory of
Jack Crompton and Brian O'Leary

AUTHOR'S PREFACE TO THE 2nd EDITION

These essays began as a project of sending weekly newsletters to my website subscribers. I wrote about subjects I myself was interested in–be they mainstream, mid-stream or far-out–and related them to my personal experiences in a somewhat autobiographical fashion.

After one year I stopped writing the newsletter (I didn't want to get in trouble with the law or anything) but my audience wanted more. They kept *nudging* me (think Yiddish) until I collected their favorites together in this book.

Few people have time for War and Peace-sized tomes anymore, but they still want quality and substance. My personal preference is for substance that's slightly subversive. (Now, if you're going to go out and abuse the substance, that's on you–I can't be responsible.)

My hope is that Curious readers will swallow this *red pill* of a book, essay by essay. The Especially Curious will proceed to their computers or the library to see where all these rabbit holes go. Let's wish everyone safe journeys.

Su Terry
Cuenca, Ecuador

TABLE OF CONTENTS
Chapters may be read in any order

CHAOS

AN ANECDOTE ABOUT Buckminster Fuller's childhood hints at his future as inventor of the Dymaxion Car, the Montreal Biosphere, and other innovations of the 20th century. It seems that little Bucky was puzzled one day in grade school when his teacher drew a line on the blackboard and said it was a "straight line that extended to infinity." Bucky looked at the line. He raised his hand. He wanted to know if the teacher had ever been to infinity, and if one end of the line went there, where did the other end go? And how could the line go to infinity, when it was on the blackboard and the blackboard doesn't go to infinity? Approaching the blackboard, Bucky also pointed out the promontories and peninsulas of the jagged chalk outline that gave the lie to the word "straight." Exasperated by her pupil's irrefutable logic, the teacher finally amended her statement by saying "Well, it *represents* a straight line."

Later in life Fuller would take delight in sharing his unique worldview with laypersons and colleagues all over the planet. His perspicacious observations tended toward the literal, and served to put scientists and thinkers back on track had they chanced to veer off via the abstract truths of higher mathematics and quantum physics. The young Bucky's observation of the chalk line's ragged edges turns out to have been a harbinger of a scientific discipline called Chaos Theory that emerged several decades later.

In the 1970s theorists were becoming fascinated with the apparent randomness of certain phenomena, like plumes of smoke and the weather. Their patterns could not be predicted–or could they? As computers became faster and more powerful, scientists could use more complex data in their experiments. It soon became evident that chaos was not what everybody thought it was.

In the 1960s Mel Brooks and Buck Henry created a television series called *Get Smart*. In this show, agents Maxwell Smart and 99 worked for an outfit called Control whose main function was to foil the dastardly plots concocted by its rival organization, Kaos. This idea of the word "chaos" meaning "disorder and confusion"–and it's not a far stretch to "bad or evil"– arose a few hundred years before television, yet the connotation strays quite far from the word's original meaning.

Chaos was a Greek god. She was the very first one, she existed before Gaia, Zeus, Aphrodite, all of them. Her name meant "the Void" (*a state of non-being prior to Creation; a formless state.*) Many great thinkers of history–Hesiod, Heraclitus, Aristotle, Ovid, the Bible authors, the Medieval alchemists– yearned to be simpatico with the great goddess.

When Chaos came to represent disorder she was demoted quite a bit. Instead of Queen of the Void, she was the disrupter who worked against godly orderliness. Still a classy dame though, she hung around like Chanel No. 5, reminding scientists there were many things they had yet to understand. Oh sure, they knew all about planetary orbits, they could tell you when the next eclipse was going to be, and when Halley's Comet would be dropping by for tea. They could make charts of the tides, and the exact times of sunrises and sunsets. Those charts and timetables were not fact, however. They were predictions, based on the rules originally laid out by Isaac Newton in the 17th century.

It just didn't seem fair that the movements of the planets, the sun, and the moon could be predicted with such accuracy, yet nobody could tell you if it was going to rain on Saturday! A meteorologist named Edward Lorenz began studying this very problem. In 1960 he worked out a weather simulation program on a huge, ungainly Royal McBee computer that was stuffed into his office at MIT. In the process of analyzing the data that came through, Lorenz made an astounding discovery: the seeming unpredictability of weather was a myth–sort of.

What we called chaos was actually a deterministic series, but there was a catch–the series could only be determined perfectly if the initial conditions were understood in their entirety. The problem was how to understand those conditions. Conditions such as the air temperature and atmospheric pressure present when a certain butterfly in a certain location flaps its wings on a certain day at a certain time, having just drunk its fill of milkweed nectar–

or not. Hence the title of Lorenz's 1969 presentation to the American Association for the Advancement of Science: "Does the Flap of a Butterfly's Wings in Brazil Set Off a Tornado in Texas?"

In any chain of events, a minuscule change at the beginning that causes a drastic change later is now known as the Butterfly Effect. When duplicating the Butterfly Effect in the lab for experimentation purposes, small deviations are deliberately introduced near the beginning of a calculation. These deviations reproduce exponentially in the system, creating a different scenario each time. On the other hand, if you can duplicate the conditions exactly, you can actually recreate a so-called chaotic pattern–proving that what we perceive as disorder actually does have an order if you go deep enough.

James Gleick, in his 1987 book *Chaos: Making a New Science*, comments "Sensitive dependence on initial conditions was not an altogether new notion," and he uses the following bit of folklore to illustrate the idea:

For want of a nail the shoe was lost
For want of a shoe, the horse was lost
For want of a horse, the rider was lost
For want of a rider, the battle was lost
For want of a battle, the kingdom was lost

Our ancestors didn't need Chaos Theory to tell them "life is what happens to you when you're busy making other plans." In modern times, you may not have a horse to shoe, but it's probably a good idea to check the air pressure in your tires before you go on a long trip.

All the stars of Chaos Theory are in Gleick's book, from Lorenz to Mandelbrot, the father of fractals. Mandelbrot came up with the idea of fractals while engaged in the problem of measuring the coastline of Britain. He realized that the closer you got, the more detail there was. And the more detail, the more coastline there was. His answer to the question "how long is the coastline of Britain" would have pleased Buckminster Fuller–"it depends on how closely you look."

Scientists are able to measure the patterns of planets, comets and tides because these are linear phenomena–their trajectories flow relatively smoothly along planes that are easily plotted on a graph. In contrast, movements of fluids, gases and stock markets are non-linear; they are not sequential or straightforward.

If we zoom out far enough though, we can see the order in chaos, in retrospect as it were. But we're not so advanced at doing the opposite–making chaos predictable. (Attention, stock analysts! I've got good news and bad news: the good news is, just because something is non-linear doesn't mean it's random! The bad news is, it might as well be.)

Chaos Theory, then, shows us there is organization where we always thought there was none. Isn't this rather comforting? It's as if some Cosmic Santa Claus said, *Yes, Virginia, there is an Order to the Universe.*

Can we not, in light of this revelation, aspire to heights of personal clarity that would allow us to perceive this order–if not 24/7, how about once in a while? 'Tis a consummation devoutly to be wished.

♪

THE DISAPPEARANCE OF PROFESSOR THEREMIN

MAYBE YOU'VE NEVER HEARD OF Professor Leon Theremin, but you've most likely heard his Frankenstein's monster of a musical instrument. Like the saxophone (named after Adolphe Sax who patented it in 1846), the theremin bears the name of its creator. The instrument looks like a rectangular box with two antennas, one on either side, and is purely electronic. The oscillators within the box create a tone whose pitch can be manipulated with one hand as it moves in front of the antenna, and its volume with the other hand. The interesting thing about the theremin is that it is played without actually touching it!

When I was around 10 a woman came to my school to demonstrate the theremin during an assembly. Lucky me–I was chosen to go up to the stage and give it a try! The screeches that I produced were a fairly accurate, if unintentional, musical portrait of Feeding Time at the Zoo. Playing the theremin felt like trying to put a leash on a giraffe and take it for a walk.

In my reverie, I fantasize that the woman who came to my school with the theremin might have been the great virtuoso Clara Rockmore. Her ability on this instrument is legendary. Moreover, Rockmore had studied with Professor Theremin himself.

Leon Theremin, born Lev Sergeyevitch Termen in St. Petersburg, Russia in 1896, had been living in the United States since 1927. He was inventing electronic musical instruments (sponsored by a wealthy patron), and had married his second wife, Lavinia Williams, a member of the American Negro Ballet. What did they have in common, the professional ballerina and the eccentric Russian inventor? Their marriage was not to last, but not for the usual reasons: in 1938, Professor Leon Theremin vanished. The controversy over his disappearance has never been satisfactorily resolved, as some say he was kidnapped from his New York apartment by the NKVD (an earlier incarnation of the KGB) and others insist he left the U.S. because of financial difficulties. It seems clear, however, that upon his return to Russia, he was indeed imprisoned in a Siberian gulag by Stalin. Theremin was then relocated to a secret research lab, where he developed electronic espionage devices. He was finally released in 1947, but continued to work as a researcher for the KGB. In 1964 he became a professor of acoustics at the Moscow Conservatory.

Communications of the day not being what they are today–the Cold War notwithstanding–no one had heard hide nor hair of the good Professor for almost thirty years until the U.S. correspondent Harold Schonberg spotted him while on assignment in Moscow in 1967. As a result of Schonberg's article in the New York Times, Theremin was dismissed from the Conservatory, whose Dean didn't want to be associated with electronic music. The news that Professor Theremin had re-surfaced was a welcome shock to the West, however. Since the Professor's disappearance, the era of electronic music he had brought forth had been growing, and mutating. His monster machine had attached itself to popular consciousness via soundtracks to films like *The Day the Earth Stood Still, The Lost Weekend,* and *Spellbound.*

In the hands of Clara Rockmore, the theremin was a gorgeous and otherworldly classical instrument used most effectively in slower, legato pieces like Saint-Saëns' "The Swan." But the instrument's gliding articulation and haunting timbre–at times stringlike, at times voice-like–also made it the go-to axe for creators of science fiction soundtracks.

In the meantime, a fourteen-year-old inventor named Robert Moog began building theremins (they can be built from kits that are still sold today). His name became forever associated, however, with yet another new instrument: the synthesizer. The original Moog Synthesizer was to today's synths as Frankenstein's monster was to Hal, the supercomputer in *2001: A Space Odyssey.* Huge consoles with rows of inputs and outputs connected by patch cords, they were machines designed to take sound apart and put it back together any way you wanted.

In the mid 1980s I studied this type of synthesizer in a class taught by the late Lefferts Brown in his studio on Canal Street. The space was more like a mad scientist's lab than a conventional music studio. Instead of your typical piano, drum set, amps and mics, it was packed with Moog and Arp synths. With these devices you could actually make your own sound waves from scratch. Spice 'em with sawtooths, squares and triangles, fry 'em with filters, then serve up some shaw 'nuff crazy chord cuisine! Music had stuck its finger in the toaster and would never be the same again. But synth music was missing one important ingredient: an artist who could legitimize it, make it accessible and commercial, make it nice. Enter Walter Carlos.

In 1968, Carlos made an album called *Switched-On Bach*–compositions by Johann Sebastian Bach performed on the synth. SOB, as it came to be known, immediately sold a half million copies and made Carlos a celebrity. Fame came with a price, however. As Carlos' career blossomed, the world demanded to know how it was that Walter Carlos of the first albums and Wendy Carlos of the later albums were one and the same person. In a famous Playboy Magazine interview, Wendy Carlos told the full story of her childhood as a secret cross dresser who always felt like a girl in a boy's body. Inspired by the stories of Renee Richards and Christine Jorgensen, Carlos had decided to undergo a sex change operation.

Though this period for Carlos was not without its complications, she never regretted making the dramatic decision to [literally] re-invent herself. She remains a well-respected composer today by virtue of a career move that solidified her reputation: In 1972, Carlos' producer and friend Rachel Elkind had heard that Stanley Kubrick was directing a new film. Being Kubrick fans and intuiting that Carlos' music would be just right for the project, they contacted Kubrick's agent and offered to send samples. Days later, Carlos and Elkind were on their way to London to plan the soundtrack for *A Clockwork Orange*.

CUE THEREMIN MUSIC–Cut to Professor Leon Theremin, returning to the United States in 1991 for a visit. Finally freed from the steel grip of the Iron Curtain, he spoke candidly with Steven Martin about his incarceration in Russia, in Martin's 1993 documentary *Theremin: An Electronic Odyssey*. Professor Theremin died in Moscow the day after the film's debut in Great Britain.

If Charlie Parker, Dizzy Gillespie and Thelonious Monk were bebop's Holy Trinity, then Theremin, Moog and Carlos are no less in the world of electronic music. Figures like these remind us, in our era of "multi-culti" education, that art is not created by cultures but by individuals. So let us not dim the bulbs of our future Birds, Dizzys, Moogs and Carloses. Let's allow them to shine, and the resulting glow will illuminate the path before us.

♪

DREAMS

SOME DREAMS WE HAVE WHILE AWAKE, some we have while sleeping. We call our waking dreams "daydreams" and, contrary to what your fifth grade teacher said, they are crucial to our functioning as human beings.

In the 1960s a plastic surgeon named Maxwell Maltz wrote a book called *Psycho-Cybernetics*. The theories in this book have influenced many subsequent authors and thinkers, some of them quite prominent in today's Human Potential-slash-New Age Movement. The gist of Psycho-Cybernetics is this: the human brain is a goal-oriented mechanism. A goal is necessary in order for it to function properly. Maltz compares the brain to a guided missile–it seeks the target, and when it goes off course it can correct itself because the programmed goal will reset its path automatically.

Our human goals can be set in one of two ways–either by the conscious mind or the unconscious mind. A goal set by the conscious mind may be quite different from a goal desired by the unconscious–not because of the content, but because the unconscious is more able to tune in to the channel of the Innermost Self. (Keeping in mind that occasionally the Innermost Self bakes a cake and something jumps out screaming "Surprise!")

Daydreams are a way to unite the conscious and the unconscious toward achieving a personal goal. When one is truly immersed in a daydream, one can actually use it to help direct one's life. Case in point: the author Napoleon Hill, who wrote the entrepreneur bible *Think and Grow Rich*, goes into great detail about his process of invoking the spirits of his idols (Abraham Lincoln, Charles Darwin, Thomas Edison, Napoleon, etc.) for imagined conferences. Hill used the creative act of daydreaming to not only sit amongst great thinkers of the past, but also to call upon them for advice! If we really do live in a holographic universe, as many scientists have suggested, then such a process seems perfectly natural. It even begs the question, why isn't everyone doing it? That the original Mr. Finance devotes so much space to esoteric techniques and spiritual philosophizing only gives him more credibility, to my mind.

Carl Jung used the process of *active imagination* (in other words, daydreaming) to mentally experience the events he later depicted in his famous *Red Book*. Since the human nervous system cannot distinguish between a real event and an event that is vividly imagined, there's much potential for using the imagination to re-program one's habitual views and behaviors. Even the word "daydream" is apropos, because a daydream is not far removed from the types of dreams one has while asleep. Of the latter, we can think of several categories, including (but not limited to) anxiety dreams (for me: looking for the missing pieces of my clarinet); nightmares; clairvoyant dreams; lucid dreams, and plain old crazy dreams that reflect one's thoughts of the day in a fun house mirror.

Of these, the type that has garnered the most attention in recent years is the lucid dream, characterized by the dreamer's realization that he is dreaming. Advanced lucid dreamers are able to go one–or many–steps further, and actually direct the course of the dream while in the awareness of the *dreaming body*. Much of Carlos Castaneda's work hinged on this type of dreaming practice, and authors such as Victor Sanchez have elucidated and expanded the idea, making it much more accessible. Another star of the lucid dreaming camp is a young Briton named Reece Jones. Jones has dedicated much of his life to exploring the various states of dream consciousness, and has categorized and documented them in a remarkable series of YouTube videos.

Those who dislike the idea of studying from someone barely old enough to vote can look to senior citizen Burt Goldman for guidance. Goldman has developed a course called Quantum Jumping which combines lucid dreaming techniques with active imagination in order to extract information from one's future, or alternate, selves. If this sounds weird, it's because it is. That's why I like it.

Lucid dream devotees will also be familiar with the 2001 Richard Linklater film *Waking Life*. It's an animated film with a fantastic soundtrack of tango music. The plot–and I use the term loosely–centers on the dream adventures of the protagonist. He meets up with philosophers, anarchists, characters of all sorts–each one of whom has a lot to say.

Do dreams come from our own minds? Or from the universe? Or from someone else's mind? Regardless of the origin of our dreams, we are protected from acting out the activities we engage in while dreaming–unless we happen to have Rapid Eye Movement Behavior Disorder. Those who suffer from this malady can move about while they are totally asleep, acting out the events they are currently dreaming of–sometimes with tragic results.

One can spend one's waking hours poorly or productively, and possibly we can do the same in sleep. If one sleeps for a third of every twenty-four hour period, that leaves sixteen or so hours to be awake. After deducting hours spent on going to work, watching stupid TV shows, preparing food, cleaning, worrying about things, waiting in line at the DMV and what-have-you, that leaves little space for deepening one's spiritual self through contemplation, meditation, or prayer. When we're sleeping, though–there's a nice chunk of time we can use for self-improvement! In fact, I seem to recall an episode of *The Partridge Family* where Danny puts books under his pillow at night . . .

But shhhhhh–keep all this under your pillow, because if the Efficiency Experts get ahold of it, next thing you know it'll be all over the Internet and we'll lose our edge. Sweet dreams, everyone.

♪

THE "MY WAY KILLINGS"

IN THE PHILIPPINES there is perhaps no pastime so loved as karaoke. Singing one song with a karaoke machine costs the equivalent of ten cents, making it an affordable amusement in a country where 80% of the population earns less than $2 worth of pesos per day. The Filipino culture values good singing, and the country is full of really fine vocalists. But there is one particular song that seems to have the power to drive men not to applause, but to murder. It is the song "My Way," made famous by Frank Sinatra and covered by dozens of other artists including Elvis, Aretha, Pavarotti and Sid Vicious.

The New York Times notes "The authorities do not know exactly how many people have been killed warbling 'My Way' in karaoke bars over the years in the Philippines, or how many fatal fights it has fueled. But the news media have recorded at least half a dozen victims in the past decade and includes them in a subcategory of crime dubbed the 'My Way Killings.'"

Theories abound as to what's really behind the killings. According to the news media, the Philippines is a rather violent society, but what is it about this one particular song that has won it a Grammy Award in the category "Composition Most Likely To Result In Homicide"? Is it the litigious lyrics? The moody melodic intervals? The creepy chord progressions?

Don't laugh. In olden days, when the Church reigned supreme, the interval of the tri-tone, e.g. C to F# (as in the first two notes of "Maria" from *West Side Story*) was called the "devil's interval." Singing, playing or composing it was strictly *verboten*. Today, this interval is the very lifeblood of modern jazz and the Great American Songbook as it comprises the two most important notes of a dominant seventh chord, the 3rd and the 7th (in a C7 chord that would be E and Bb). This interval does not occur at all in the melody of "My Way," however.

The English lyrics to the song were written specifically for Sinatra by Paul Anka. In 1967 Anka heard the tune in its French version *Comme D'Habitude* (by Francois, Revaux & Thibault), and he was inspired to secure the rights to the song and compose an English lyric for his friend Frank, who at that time was depressed about his career and considering getting out of the business.

It's a pretty macho song, to say the least. But shouldn't these lyrics sublimate a desire to kill, rather than instigate it? Not necessarily, my dear Watson. When we read further into the news story mentioned earlier, we discover that most of the deaths were perpetrated by an audience member who was angered by the singer's poor rendition of the song. Now that's more like it! If only crappy performers were ALWAYS killed before they could harm the ears of innocent victims!

The killings usually take place in bars. Karaoke and alcohol: a dangerous mix. Surely there are hundreds of songs that have been maimed or slaughtered due to lack of a Designated Singer. And what is it about "My Way," in particular, that itches the trigger finger? This is where your intrepid reporter jumped into the fray with her high-tech audio equipment–namely, a Numark DJ turntable with a reverse control.

Whoa–back up. What's this about a reverse control, and why do we need one? For starters, let's double park on Memory Lane, corner of Rue d' 1968: The Beatles song "Revolution #9" played backwards revealed the words "turn me on dead man." Similarly, the song "I'm So Tired" (also from *The White Album*) when played backwards sounded like "Paul is a dead man, miss him, miss him, miss him." This is a technique known as *backmasking* in recording studio parlance, and it became the focus of a fight between Christian audio vigilantes and the rock groups of the day. The decline of vinyl–and the phonograph–and the birth of the compact disc succeeded in quelling the controversy since CD players don't run in reverse. The phenomenon lives on, however, in the work of David Oates of Australia, founder of Reverse Speech Technologies. He has devoted his life to studying the hidden messages in reverse speech and lyrics.

So I reverse-played Sinatra's version of "My Way" from *The Main Event* album, recorded live at Madison Square Garden in 1974, to see if there might be any hidden Satanic messages in there. (I didn't detect any, but I may pass it on to Mr. Oates just to make sure.) Rather, I think the power of the song lies in four things:

• A melodic line that keeps ascending. This is very effective.
• Just the right proportion of tension and release in the harmonic structure (the chords), ending in a major key.
• The melody tells a story and so do the words. It's a universal story that people over 40 or 50 can relate to–we've spent decades facing life's challenges.
• Sinatra's unique delivery, which put the stamp on the song and imprinted it into the Collective Unconscious. Is there anyone left on the planet who hasn't heard this tune?

       And let's not forget:
• The rousing band arrangement by Don Costa. Okay, five things.

MY WAY
By Jacques Revaux, Claude Francois, Giles Thibault
English lyric by Paul Anka

And now the end is near
And so I face the final curtain
My friend I'll make it clear
I'll state my case of which I'm certain
I've lived a life that's full
Traveled each and every highway
And more, much more than this
I did it my way
Regrets I've had a few
But then again too few to mention
I did what I had to do
And saw it through without exception
I planned each charted course
Each careful step along the byway
And more, much more than this
I did it my way
Yes there were times I guess you knew
When I bit off more than I could chew
But through it all when there was doubt
I ate it up and spit it out
I grew tall through it all
and did it my way
I've loved, I've laughed and cried
I've had my fill, my share of losing

14

But now as tears subside
I find it all so amusing
To think I did all that
And may I say not in a shy way
Oh no, oh no, not me
I did it my way
For what is a man what has he got
If not himself then he has naught
To say the things he truly feels
And not the words of one who kneels
The record shows I took the blows
And did it my way

Music may be one of the most powerful forces in existence. It has the demonstrable ability to bring together vast numbers of people toward a common goal. Composer George M. Cohan was awarded the Congressional Gold Medal (the highest civilian award, along with the Presidential Medal of Freedom) because of songs like "You're a Grand Old Flag" and "Over There" that lifted the morale of U.S. soldiers and citizens during WW I. The 1985 single "We Are The World," by Michael Jackson and Lionel Richie, raised over $63 million for humanitarian aid. The national anthem of one's country, whether performed in a huge arena or a school gymnasium, imbues people with pride and patriotism.

Church hymns, folk songs, operatic arias, Country & Western ballads–they all push our buttons, working us just like the bell on Pavlov's dog. If you doubt that songs evoke memories, feelings and primal urges, just ask the advertising execs who bring you the jingles you hear every day on radio and TV. You know you look better in a sweater washed in Woolite!

If you count every Sinatra song that sweethearts danced to, that lonely men drank to, that rogues whistled and Romeos whispered, you might even say that Ol' Blue Eyes had more power than any President. And his term was longer. Even now, years after he left us, he's still calling the shots.

♪

ALASKA ADVENTURE • PART I

THE SKY IS A DOME over us. Boating on Kachemak Bay, we're floating on top of the Earth. 360 degree views as far as the eye can see. Sea otters are frolicking, holding their pups on their bellies with one fin while they swim on their backs. A lone seal. Bunches, no, hordes of cormorants and murres sitting on a giant rock that is partially constructed of their own excrement. Smells like it. And mountains, mountains, mountains, covered with snowy rivulets, framing the lovely scene of which we are part.

The day lasts forever; it won't get even a little dark until 3 a.m. We see bald eagles. Harmon comments that the eagle is a mean bird that swoops down on its prey, showing no mercy. Someone says, "The eagle is the national bird of the United States." Someone else says "Hmmmmmmmm."

Later, two more eagles perch on the tops of the highest trees directly across from the lodge. They watch us as we take the outboard-fitted rowboat across the cove, to the boardwalk that surrounds the Saltry Restaurant, the art gallery, and several homes.

We meet the locals on our way down to the gravel beach. Untold numbers of arrowheads and other items, thousands of years old, are regularly found there. Why are we here? Because a couple months before, pianist Peggy Stern had called me up and said "You wanna go to Alaska?"

"You bet," I had replied. It would be my first time visiting our 49th state, though it was Peggy's fourth tour there. She became our official guide as we flew first to Seattle then to Anchorage on a Boeing 737, continuing on to Homer, Alaska on a 37-seat de Havilland Dash 8 Turboprop. As I remarked to my Twitter followers, it's not often you get a flight attendant with 45 years experience!

Peggy and I were accompanied by our respective significant others, John and Gil. The four of us were met at the Homer airport by our hosts Pauli and Harmon Hall, proprietors of the Quiet Place Lodge. They were the organizers of the concerts and workshops we did, and their lodge was to be our home for one wonderful week. But first we had to get there , so we boarded their vessel *Dragonfly* and made our way across Kachemak Bay to Halibut Cove, about a twenty minute ride.

Halibut Cove is a small community of part-timers and a few full-time residents who live in raised-up houses along the shore. Daily transportation is by boat, and even the Hall's twelve-year-old son Ian has his own–a motorized skiff with fearsome shark's jaws painted on the bow. All boats have names, and Ian's is *Bruce*–no one knows why. Ian comes and goes several times a day, visiting his friends and running the occasional errand for his parents, who operate the lodge during the short Alaska summer.

The main lodge features a full cook's kitchen, living and dining areas, and bathroom. There are separate buildings with a library and laundry room as well as a sauna. Several cabins for guests and staff are situated on the surrounding decks. The docks and boathouses along the perimeter of the cove are all on floats, with ramps connecting to the decks and homes up above. At low tide, one trudges up the ramp at a 45 degree angle; at high tide it's almost parallel with the water below, as the floats and ramps follow the tide's slow roll.

Areas such as these, so intertwined with the environment not only in lifestyle but also in livelihood, display a pristine appearance to visitors. The color of the water is a deep forest green with a marine tint. I did not see one piece of trash anywhere.

If I were Russia, I would be really sorry that I sold *Alyeska* to us for two cents an acre back in 1867. Especially after the oil boom arising from the discovery of major reserves in Prudhoe Bay, on the northernmost coast, in 1968. Petroleum extraction accounts for a large percentage of the state's income, so it's no wonder that this is the front lines in our country's war of Economic Development vs. Natural Resource Preservation.

Our hosts Pauli and Harmon met each other in 1989 while each worked a job connected with the Exxon Valdez oil spill cleanup. That spill did much damage in the Gulf of Alaska, and residents felt the pain of their compatriots in the Gulf of Mexico who suffered an oil spill of their own twenty years later. That spill, resulting from the explosion at BP's Deepwater Horizon oil rig, captured national attention to the point where President Obama's administration made it illegal for journalists to approach within 65 feet of any cleanup activity, as reported by Anderson Cooper of CNN.

As noted on BP's own website, their main weapons in managing the cleanup were dispersal of the oil and reclamation of the oil. Cynics amongst us will also note that the dispersant product was one of the least effective in current use. It had the advantage, however, of being manufactured by a company named Nalco with proven ties to the oil industry. So it wasn't likely that other suggestions (such as using hay as an absorbent, or using oil-eating microbes) would ever be utilized.

While solutions like the latter may seem overly simplistic, lately I am sensing a high degree of acceptance amongst Americans for simple solutions to complex problems, even in our current high-tech age. Popular culture illustrates this point. Honest and down-to-earth film characters like Forrest Gump and Chauncey Gardiner, with their bull-busting wisdom, have become icons in our society. And in real life, the highly intellectual yet infinitely clear-minded 14th Dalai Lama (the exiled spiritual leader of the Tibetan people) is practically a rock star.

Going back to our simple roots, as it were, has spawned a host of new medicines as the pharmaceutical industry continues to package, patent, and profit from plants and herbs that have grown in the world's rainforests for millennia—and for free. As long as Profit remains the number one motivator, preservation of the earth's natural resources may depend upon those who wish to preserve them only for profit and for no other reason.

Not only in Alaska but also in the "lower 48," it seems that dependence on the oil industry has created neglect in developing the potentially vast energy supplies from hydroelectric power, wind, and geothermal technologies—even though there are presumably large profits to be made in these areas as well, and at far less cost to the environment.

In Halibut Cove we find a rugged place where survival depends upon the help of one's neighbors. One might even say, at the end of the day, it's the act of people helping people that makes a real difference in the living conditions on the entire planet.

On the great carousel of life, if money makes the world go 'round, the Zen Koan du jour may be: If the carousel goes 'round and no one is there to hear it, will it still make a sound?

♪

ALASKA ADVENTURE • PART II

MY FAMILY MOVED FROM OHIO to Connecticut when I was nine years old. Coming from a flat, relatively-treeless town in the Buckeye State to a woodsy enclave in the hilly Nutmeg State was environment shock of the first order.

When we drove into our new neighborhood for the first time, my mother pointed out the corner where I would wait for the school bus. Gadzooks–we were in the middle of the forest! Anxiety wracked my small body as I wondered how on earth I would ever find the bus stop again, with so many trees around. *I know*, I told myself. *I'll just look for the little clearing in the woods!* Soon enough I realized that the bus stop was just at the end of our dirt road.

I came to love being surrounded by woods and grew up exploring them at every opportunity. There was one thing that puzzled me though–there were stone walls everywhere you turned. They looked really old. Who built them, and why? Turns out the stones had been deposited by what adults referred to as The Glacier. Back in the 18th century walls had been constructed with the stones, to mark property lines and contain animals as the land was cleared for farming.

I couldn't comprehend a mass of ice so gargantuan that it could gather up billions of rocks, releasing them to the earth as it melted. Not to mention leaving behind a pile of dirt that is today known as Long Island. (I'm sure Long Islanders would prefer not to think of their home turf as Connecticut's leftovers-but there you have it.) What does all this have to do with Alaska, you ask? Hold your horses, I'm getting to that.

As a kid, I thought that glaciers had something to do with the Ice Age and were basically extinct. When global warming became a hot topic, once again glaciers entered the conversation because people said they were melting. As the debate over whether glaciers should be allowed to melt waged onward, I despaired of ever actually seeing one before they'd be puddled into submission by devastating greenhouse gas attacks. But in Alaska (finally, the point!) I saw not just one glacier, but two–in person!

Grewingk Glacier is thirteen miles long. The approach to its base is a four-mile-long trek along a gravel beach, then a forest leading to a well-trod path through scrub and sparse trees to a beach opposite the lake at the glacier's bottom. Nothing could have prepared me for the sight of this magnificent display. One stands awestruck and silent at the majesty of it. You look at images like this in coffee table books and think how wonderful it would be to see them someday, not really believing you ever will.

Floating in the lake are huge chunks of ice that have become detached and rolled down the glacier. They have sections that are the brightest aquamarine blue you've ever seen. The color results from the compression of the ice over time, which squeezes the oxygen out. The density of the ice absorbs all the colors of the spectrum except blue, which is reflected.

Scientists study the history of the earth by analyzing geological, chemical, and paleontological evidence. Variations in isotopes of fossils in sedimentary rock are measured and compared. Bubbles of entrapped air in glaciers reveal carbon dioxide and methane concentrations while also supplying data on atmospheric temperatures throughout history.

The dispersion of fossils shows which parts of the earth were connected once upon a time, and where they where on the globe. For instance: During the Triassic Period (200-250 million years ago), the land mass we call Connecticut was located much further south, enjoying a sub-tropical climate similar to Central America all year 'round. At the beginning of this era, known as the Permian Period, the few parts of Alaska that were already formed were located near the equator! New Jersey was buying gas in Morocco, by virtue of being its next door neighbor in the supercontinent known as Pangaea. Likewise, the rest of the world at that time was one giant ocean, which scientists refer to as Panthalassa. It wasn't until the Cretaceous Period (about 145 to 65 million years ago) that Pangaea began to break apart into the continents we recognize today. It seems the field of geology is the perfect embodiment of the Buddhist principle of impermanence!

Popular culture makes reference to The Ice Age as if there were only one. Science, however, deems an ice age to be any time period during which ice sheets, such as the ones in Greenland and Antarctica, exist on the earth. Technically, therefore, we are in an ice age right now.

The warming process proceeds at a glacial pace; the retreat of ice sheets and glaciers begun between 15,000 and 18,000 years ago is still going on, allowing us to experience a warmer earth for the time being. But not all the earth's glaciers are retreating. For instance, Alaska's Hubbard Glacier–the largest tidewater glacier in North America–has been advancing for over a century.

As any geeky geology website will explain, for at least a billion years the earth has been passing alternately through ice ages and warming ages–emphasis on the ice. Perhaps as Geek Culture has become more trendy (as evidenced by TV ads like Verizon's, featuring the guy with the thick black eyeglasses and the cool walkie-talkie), mainstream news has taken the cue to recognize the other side of the controversy. Hence the switch in buzzwords from "global warming" to "climate change." That lets media pundits sit on the fence a while longer before they recommend exchanging bikinis for parkas.

The truth is that no one knows for sure where the earth's thermometer is headed. Human agendas come and go, usually following the money trail. In any case, one needs only to witness (hopefully not in person) an earthquake, tsunami, volcanic eruption, hurricane, avalanche, flood, lightning strike, etc., to be convinced that in any major struggle of Man against Nature, all bets are off. But if we MUST go there–the smart money is on The Planet.

♪

FEAR

WHEN I WAS A KID my family lived on a dirt road that wasn't quite a dead end, but it terminated with a steep hill rutted with so many potholes that no vehicle ever ventured onto it. In the winter, this hill became the neighborhood sledding course. We named it Dead Man's Hill–or maybe only I called it that. Because while all the other kids were saying "Yay, let's go sledding!" I was willing my record collection and my Kurt Vonnegut books to my little brother. I'd grimly pull on my snow boots, say goodbye to my mother, and make sure I had on clean underwear for what would surely be my last day on earth. And I had another fear that was even greater than that of sledding down Dead Man's Hill, and that was the fear of hating myself if I wasn't brave enough to do it. Come to find out, decades later, I'm not alone: even OLYMPIC ATHLETES are in the same boat.

"Everybody feels fear out there, and I mean everybody," says Ross Hindman (founder of the International Snowboard Training Center, located in Colorado and California) in a recent New York Times article. The article goes on to mention a new study by New York University postdoctoral fellow Daniela Schiller, in which she explains the old theory of "getting back on the horse" in modern, scientific terms. According to Schiller, "you have only a short window in which a memory is vulnerable to revision." During this window, you can physically get back on the horse, or you can replay the event in your mind, altering it through the process of imagination to turn a painful memory into a positive one. But if you wait too long, the negative memory is "returned to long term brain storage" and your chance is lost. Well darn, if that isn't exactly what Grandma used to say!

While some people may think that getting up on stage and playing improvised saxophone solos in front of an audience should be terrifying, I guess that never bothered me. My childhood fear of severe physical injury, however, has never left, even though I force myself to face it regularly. Over the years, I've repeatedly challenged myself by engaging in a number of dangerous sports. Many of my adventures took place with my dear friends George

Vinick and Margaret Saxe who served as guides and mentors. These adventures included skydiving, white water canoeing, back country Nordic skiing over frozen rivers and rock climbing, among others.

After getting my first Conquering Fear merit badges from George and Margaret, I started to venture out on my own. On a trip to New Mexico I belayed off of cliffs, did a ropes course, and rode a horse blindfolded. (The blindfold was on me, not the horse.) On a trip to Finland, I rode a horse at breakneck speed through the forest, trying to keep up with my guide who was helpfully showing me how much fun you could have in her country. I squeezed my legs against the horse's belly as tightly as possible so as not to hit the trees. Afterwards, I couldn't walk for a week. Accustomed to Western riding, I remember my dismay at having to wear that stupid English riding hat, which in retrospect seems like a rather good idea.

The ultra-scariest thing I ever did was firewalking. This was also in New Mexico, on a separate trip. It was part of a conference put on by spiritual teacher and author Stuart Wilde. The firewalking path was set up in the hotel parking lot. During the day, while the fire was burning down to the red-hot coals, the firewalking expert led a four-hour workshop during which we practiced facing our fears, whatever they were, and symbolically tossing them out. At the end of the workshop we practiced a dry-run on the carpet, pretending that we were walking over hot coals instead of tufted wool.

Participants also had the choice of not walking over the coals, but you had to make a definite decision one way or the other. The workshop leader made the point that whether you chose to walk or not walk, your decision was respected if it was a choice you made and not something you did because others were doing it, or that you didn't do because you were afraid.

Just in case you're tempted to take a cavalier attitude during the workshop and say *it's all in the mind, no problem*, the guy keeps reminding you, in graphic detail, what happens to people with fourth degree burns. The point being, you must make your choice based on reality and not fantasy.

Firewalking is traditional in many countries—even in– Greece! People who've never done firewalking try to say it's a trick. They say perspiration on your feet protects you from being burned, or that the coals aren't really that hot. Riiiiiiight. My feet are extremely sensitive. One time when I was on tour someone stole my shoes on a beach in Guadeloupe, and I couldn't traverse an asphalt parking lot to get back to my room. The sailing instructor ended up carrying me across–slightly embarrassing. So I know what hot is. Trust me, the coals are hot.

The feeling of empowerment following the ceremony was palpable. The room was buzzing with energy as people shared their experiences. On 5x7 index cards, those of us who walked wrote the words *I walked on fire. I can do anything I choose.*

What I've discovered about fear is that if I don't continually examine it, re-imagine it, challenge it–it will rule me. Certainly fear has an important role to play as a motivator (as when outrunning the saber-toothed tiger–or the mugger), or as a warning (I normally give Mack trucks the right-of-way even when they're wrong.) But the role of fear is only that–a role. When its role is not called for, we don't need to give it a part in our lives.

I clearly remember a certain day from twenty-odd years ago. My father had been walking down the street in New York and all of a sudden he couldn't catch his breath. He was with my brother, who took him to the hospital so they could run some tests and make sure he was okay. I met my brother at the hospital and we called my mother in Connecticut, telling her what happened, reassuring her that Dad was fine and they were just checking him over. "I'm coming to the hospital," she said. About forty-five minutes later, it occurred to us that she might be better off taking a different route in order to avoid traffic. "I'm sure she's already left," my brother said.

He dialed the house, and, surprisingly, Mom picked up the phone. My brother started to tell her to take the FDR drive rather than the West Side Highway, then he looked at me, covering the mouthpiece with his hand. "She's crying," he whispered. I grabbed the phone. "Stay there Mom, we'll come and pick you up and bring you here." Even though this very strong and independent woman had driven to New York hundreds of times, fear of her husband's death rendered her completely incapable of even leaving the house.

Emotions aren't part of the rational mind, so they can't be explained away. Yet the rational mind is necessary to temper the emotions, to prevent us from acting on them inappropriately. Even so, we cannot change the way we feel. The only thing we have any control over is how we act. This is where our power lies. When we act according to a sense of morality or a code of honor, we're able to transmute the energy of negative emotions like fear, jealousy and anger into actions that not only help oneself, but also allow one to be of service to others.

It may be true that fear memories can be eliminated if they are revised immediately afterwards, during the short window mentioned earlier. But what about fear memories that have stayed with us because they were never addressed while that window was open? Are we to be forever controlled by such memories, destined to repeat detrimental patterns in our lives over and over again? Fear memories are imprinted on the energy body. Practices that allow one to access the energy body, such as meditation, yoga and t'ai chi, can help us touch those imprints, and change them. And I keep trying to change them because I'm afraid of what will happen if I don't.

The best remedy for those who are afraid, lonely or unhappy is to go outside, somewhere where they can be quiet, alone with the heavens, nature and God. Because only then does one feel that all is as it should be and that God wishes to see people happy, amidst the simple beauty of nature. –Anne Frank

Collective fear stimulates herd instinct, and tends to produce ferocity toward those who are not regarded as members of the herd. –Bertrand Russell

Experience teaches us that silence terrifies people the most. –Bob Dylan

25

You gain strength, courage, and confidence by every experience in which you really stop to look fear in the face. You must do the thing which you think you cannot do. –
Eleanor Roosevelt

Don't be afraid to go out on a limb. That's where the fruit is. –H.
Jackson Brown, Jr.

Let us not look back in anger or forward in fear, but around in awareness. –James Thurber

Our deepest fear is not that we are inadequate. Our deepest fear is that we are powerful beyond measure.
–Marianne Williamson

I fear not the man who has practiced 10,000 kicks once, but I fear the man who has practiced one kick 10,000 times. –Bruce Lee

A warrior never worries about his fear. Instead, he thinks about the wonders of seeing the flow of energy! The rest is frills, unimportant frills. –Castaneda's
Don Juan

I have learned over the years that when one's mind is made up, this diminishes fear; knowing what must be done does away with fear.
–Rosa Parks

♪

THE GREAT ACORN CAPER

HORACE KEPHART'S BOOK *Camping and Woodcraft*–in which he gives the lowdown on everything from edible plant foraging to tanning animal skins to building a cabin in the woods, was first published by Macmillan in 1917. Was it any accident that during the war years of 1939-1945 the book was reprinted four times? Perhaps in wartime people are more apt to realize that their lifestyle could be interrupted at any moment, and survival might depend upon making do with what Nature provides.

My copy of the book, given to me by a friend thirty years ago, is yellowed but intact: 479 pages of wisdom for would-be survivalists. Can't say I've actually read the whole thing, but I keep it handy for any Y2K's or 2012's that may come down the pike.

I remember a time in 1985 when I went camping with my friend Richie. We drove to a campsite in the Catskills, and I prepared camp while Richie went fishing in the lake for our dinner. Richie lived on 43rd Street in Manhattan. He did not catch any fish. So we drove to ShopRite and bought chicken parts.

Back at camp, I strung up our provisions from a tree limb, as instructed by Mr. Kephart, to keep them from bears and other varmints. Before long, a skunk wandered by to see what was up. "A skunk! Throw a rock at it!" Richie yelled. "No, don't!" he yelled again. (Living on 43rd Street sharpens the wits, enabling speed-of-light thought and rapid-fire decision-making.) The skunk split on his own recognizance, and the next day so did we. But the romantic notion of living off the land lingers on, like the scent of skunk in the night woods.

As a kid, I rode my bicycle all over the Connecticut back roads, making frequent forays into the surrounding forest. My mother had told me to never, ever, eat anything that was growing wild, so I sampled Nature's lot with the zeal only Prohibition can bring. As Horace Kephart confirms, "Not all of our wild food-plants are acrid or poisonous in a raw state, nor is it dangerous for anyone with a rudimentary knowledge of botany to experiment with them. Many are easily identified by those who know nothing at all of botany. I cannot say that all of them are palatable; but most of them are, when properly prepared for the table. Their taste in a raw state, generally speaking, is no more a criterion than is that of raw beans or asparagus."

Herein lies the rub: *their taste in a raw state . . .* This is a not-so-subtle reminder that most of the foods we eat today undergo a considerable amount of processing before being packaged (wheat and rice, for instance) and require further processing, in the form of cooking, before they are finally edible. Such is the case with the acorn. But it practically rained acorns this year, and I was not going to let all of them escape.

SHELL: Bake acorns in 200 degree oven on a cookie sheet or tray, to crack open the shells. Further crack shells by laying them on a big towel and smashing with a wide hammer, or standing on them with a hard flat surface such as a ceramic tile. You can dance if you want. Shell acorns. Discard any that have a tiny hole in the shell, or that look rotten when you open them. Use a nutcracker, hammer, or simply bite down on shell to open. This step is time consuming. I suggest having an Acorn Shelling Party, *a la* Tom Sawyer. You could also do it while listening to music, or watching a stupid TV show that has no other justification. Or you could devise an Acorn Meditation—the road to nirvana is paved with acorns.

LEACH: Taste the raw acorn meat. If it's very bitter, boil several times and drain water each time. Acorns in the White Oak family should not be very bitter. I leached mine two times only.

DEHYDRATE: Dry the wet acorn meat in a 200 degree oven, with the door open so the meat doesn't burn (about 1/2 hour). Or you can lay them out in the sun. But make sure the squirrels don't take them: *Hey, wow! Thanks!*

GRIND: Process in food processor or clean coffee grinder to a medium texture. In my Kitchen Aid this took only a few minutes of grinding. Stop and check frequently, or you'll end up with too fine a powder, or else nut butter. (History buffs will note that the first Native Americans didn't have Kitchen Aids or Cuisinarts. If anyone desires a more authentic reenactment experience, please go right ahead and grind manually!) Use the resulting acorn meal with different recipes that are in books and on the Internet. The one I adapted for my Acorn Muffins is from Euell Gibbons' book *Stalking the Wild Asparagus*, recommended by my friend Lisa Tso. I found a used copy at Powell's Books in Portland, Oregon, but it is still in print and available at Amazon.

My acorn muffins were delicious! Very hearty, not too sweet, with nice texture and a moist consistency. They're good with butter, jam, or as dinner rolls. But even more delicious was the feeling of satisfaction at harvesting my free, organic acorns. Well, I suppose they're not exactly free–but they're definitely included in my property taxes. The egg, sugar, milk, olive oil and salt I bought at the store. But in a pinch, what's stopping me from getting a hen, a cow, an olive tree? Salt . . . let's see, I think I could figure that out.

Harvesting sugar from beets may be slightly more problematic, however. The so-called "Roundup Ready" sugar beet now accounts for 95% of the United States crop. Roundup is a weed killer invented by Monsanto, the giant chemical company. As most people know, the problem with herbicides, antibiotics and insecticides is that their subjects tend to develop resistance to them. When certain weeds began showing a resistance to Roundup, Monsanto isolated the resistant gene and began inserting it into seeds, thereby creating crops that were themselves resistant to Roundup. This meant the crops could be doused with Roundup and live, while the still-evolving weeds would die. Opponents to herbicides argue that harvesting Roundup Ready crops may be a lot easier for farmers in the short term, but possibly not in the long term.

Here I cannot help but make a seemingly unrelated comparison to the music business! When musicians do a live gig, we have to *mix* the sound using microphones, amps and equalizers so the blend is good for both the audience and the musicians. The general approach to mixing is to boost the volume of any instrument that is not being heard adequately. This is the easiest way, but it often results in muddy sound with poor definition as you keep cranking the volume.

A more refined solution is to lower the volume of the instruments that are too loud. This somewhat more time-consuming process, however, combined with the fragile egos of musicians who prefer not to be turned down, makes it impractical for many situations. So we usually end up dousing everything with Soundup. The difference between Soundup and Roundup is that at the end of a gig, no damage has been done–unless you count those little cilia in the inner ear that don't survive the audio onslaught. But you don't really start missing them till you're around 60 years old, and that's so far away . . .

I could sign up my acorns as USDA Organic. That means I followed organic practices on my oak trees by not using chemicals on them. It doesn't mean, however, that my acorns are necessarily completely free from contaminants. My neighbor's chemically treated plant pollens might have been transported here by bees, wind, rain or cattle. Or a passing vehicle could have dropped some genetically modified seed on my property.

Farmers who don't use genetically modified seed find their crops are often contaminated with GM pollen from other farms in the area. Monsanto has been the defendant in some anti-trust suits because of its Microsoft-like history of buying up the major seed companies (to the tune of $9 billion) and hard-selling bundled packages of GM seeds and herbicides to farmers. Their "loyalty program" then rewards farmers who use at least 70% Monsanto seeds. The farmers also must agree to use only Roundup as their herbicide, rather than a competing product. It's brilliant, actually: get people to buy a problem, then sell them the solution.

In today's controversial food industry saga, Monsanto is not the only villain. Other players make appearances in the recent film *Food, Inc.*, which does for the food industry what Upton Sinclair's *The Jungle* did for the meat packing industry a hundred years ago.

In the year 2000, the World Health Organization ranked the U.S. 37th in the list of health care performance amongst 191 countries. As author Michael Pollan points out, "more than half of what we spend on health care–of that $2.5 trillion—is going [towards treating] preventable, chronic diseases linked to diet."

Until the food business becomes more about food and less about business (and similarly for health care) the consumer will continue to get the short end of the stick. This is ironic, because it is actually the consumer who holds more power–at least collectively. The only reason so-called "health foods" arrived in supermarkets at all is because consumers demanded them.

Unfortunately, as long as healthy food choices are tied to a higher price point, many people will not be able to afford the choice. But you can always go to the park and collect acorns! Not to mention the rest of the vast array of foods found in backyards, meadows, parking lots, and by the side of the road.

Read my bumper: *I Brake For Foragers.*

AUNTIE SU'S ORGANIC ACORN MUFFINS

Sift together:
1 c bread flour
1 c acorn meal
3 TBS sugar
3 tsp baking powder
1 tsp salt

Beat one egg. Mix in 3/4 cup half n half, 1/4 cup water, and 3 TBS olive oil. Mix wet ingredients with dry till everything is moist. Pour into greased muffin tins. Bake at 400 degrees for 20 minutes. If you use a greased loaf pan for acorn bread, bake at 400 degrees for 30 minutes.

♪

THE KING AND THE PAWN

CHESS: THE ULTIMATE GAME of strategy, played the world over. Unlike other sports, its field of battle invites all worthy warriors to duel, whether male or female, 10 years old or 90. In its original form, the game dates back to 6th century India. Chess as we know it today began in Europe in the 16th century, and the current rules date from the 19th century.

I haven't played chess for quite a while; but I do like thinking about it, and I'm not the only one, apparently. Over the years many types of symbols have been philosophically overlaid onto chess, including those of war, cosmology, astrology, numerology, metaphysics, and sex. Many musicians are fans of the game (Jazz legends Dizzy Gillespie, Max Roach and Art Blakey, among others, were chess players).

These days I'm zooming out, getting the big picture on a lot of subjects I focused on in detail years earlier. From this standpoint, two chess pieces hold a particular fascination for me: the king and the pawn. These pieces have entered our world as archetypes. As such, one can gain insights into life by contemplating them. It's not unlikely that this is exactly what the inventors of the game had in mind when they created it.

The functions of certain ancient monuments, for example, were at one time taken very literally: The pyramids? Oh yeah, they were tombs for the Pharaohs. Stonehenge? Burial ground. Chartres Cathedral? Beautiful church. As anyone who watches the Discovery Channel knows, however, scholars have shown us there are many more layers to these realities. The fact is, much of the meaning invested in objects and rituals from antiquity is not readily apparent. This is entirely appropriate–truth reveals itself only to those who seek it.

When certain medieval alchemists attempted to transmute lead into gold it was not physical gold, but spiritual gold they sought. One can imagine that the elegant game of chess, too, may have been imbued with hidden meanings. Of course, almost anything can be thought of in this way, i.e. having another meaning besides the merely literal. Take my field of jazz music, for instance. To a fan, perhaps it's just groovy sounds; to a connoisseur, it can be a miniature journey paralleling the vicissitudes of life.

Let us begin our meditation on chess with The King. Although conventional wisdom says that the King symbolizes the spirit or heart of a person, I believe it would be more accurately related to the ego–the part of Self which believes it is in command. The ego is an essential part of ourselves, for it's the part that dares to present one's being to the world at large. It's the part that says *I exist*. In the extraordinary system of checks and balances that is the human psyche, we have other parts of Self that say things like *no, you don't*. Those parts aren't good at debating, though, so sometimes they just have to wait around until the ego gets temporarily crushed (*I wouldn't go out with you if you were the last guy on earth*) before they can assert themselves.

My theory of King-as-Ego derives not from whimsy, but from the rules of chess themselves. The king has little power of his own. He cannot usually capture an opposing piece because he doesn't have the range of movement. Therefore, he must be protected by every other piece. There is even a special move called *castling*, where the king and the rook may move at the same time to safeguard the king. Likewise, the ego, too, must be protected. We do this with psychological pieces called defense mechanisms. In chess, one cannot actually capture or kill the king, but one can make it impossible for him to move. (One cannot kill the ego–but one can take away its power to command the Self.) This is checkmate, the end of the game.

At the other end of the chessboard hierarchy we have the lowly pawn. The literary expression "a mere pawn," though, belies the true potential of this piece. For it is the ONLY piece that, should it make it all the way across the board, acquires the power to change into a Queen, Knight, Bishop or Rook. The chess term for this is *promotion*.

The journey across life's chessboard is full of pitfalls, pratfalls and predators. For me, the pawn's movements symbolize our true potential as humans. Unlike the other pieces, the pawn can only move in a forward direction. On its journey it may venture far from its king, who (except when castling) may move only one square at a time. The pawn–the individual–who reaches the eighth rank (the other side) acquires the understanding of himself and the universe that lets him transform himself.

Then again, maybe the phrase *merely a pawn* is accurate because the pieces are not playing by themselves-someone higher up is directing them. On an interior level, what part of Self is this? It's the Essential Self, the core. This is the part that knows what we're supposed to be doing with our lives. Although it is mute, it often speaks to us in dreams with its own symbolic language. The pawn shows that the only important thing is focusing on the goal and moving slowly and steadily towards it.

As of this writing, the reigning world chess champion is Magnus Carlsen of Norway, born in 1990. In a Time Magazine article from January 2010, Carlsen said that he can see fifteen to twenty moves ahead, but stressed that he does not rely solely on logic to determine his course of action. According to Garry Kasparov, a former world champion, Carlsen's command of the game is intuitive. Often called the Mozart of chess, Carlsen "has a natural feel for where to place the pieces." The Time article goes on to say "Carlsen has a knack for sensing the potential energy in each move, even if its ultimate effect is too far away for anyone, even a computer, to calculate. In the Grandmaster commentary room, where chess's clerisy gather to analyze play, the experts did not even consider several of Carlsen's moves during his game with [champion Vladimir] Kramnik until they analyzed them and realized they were perfect. 'It's hard to explain,' Carlsen says. 'Sometimes a move just feels right.'"

Carlsen's female counterpart is Judit Polgar of Hungary. Even after a period of retirement to raise her children, she is universally acknowledged as the greatest female player of all time. In 1991 she achieved the rank of Grandmaster at age 15–becoming the youngest Grandmaster in history, breaking Bobby Fischer's record by one month. She has beaten many world champions, including Viswanathan Anand, Kasparov, and Carlsen. Along with her two sisters (who are almost as good at chess as she is) Judit was home-schooled by her father Laszlo in chess, math, and languages. At 10 years old she was reducing male grownup opponents to jelly, playing with her teddy bear while they were trying to figure out their next move.

I doubt that Carlsen, Polgar, and other chess champs think much about the symbolism of the game. They just play. And practice. They leave the symbolism to us armchair philosophers who don't take up the game but sign our kids up for lessons.

In case anyone is thinking kids can learn just as much from playing video games, writer and chess player Zac Taylor has a few words for you: "In the first move of a chess game, White has exactly twenty possible moves available to him. Black has the same number . . . twenty multiplied by twenty is four hundred, which is the exact number of positions that a chess board can have after white and black play their very first moves . . . on move two, the number of possible chess positions exceeds the number of people living in Raleigh, North Carolina . . . by move six, the number of possible positions exceeds the number of stars in the universe."

Take that, Tetris.

♪

LIFE IN THE OUTBACK

BILL PHILLIPS GAVE ME A BOOK called *Mutant Message Down Under* which purports to be a quasi-autobiographical tale of an American woman going on walkabout with a tribe of Aborigines in Australia in the 1980s. The book was quite controversial when it came out in the early 1990s, rather on the order of the brouhaha surrounding Carlos Castaneda in the decades prior: Truth, or fiction?

My take on Carlos Castaneda, a prior exponent of non-ordinary reality, is that it doesn't matter whether or not the stories are true because the teachings within are valid regardless of the veracity of the events in the books. I feel the same way about Marlo Morgan's *Mutant Message*.

The Australian Aboriginal culture–between 40,000 and 60,000 years old–is the oldest continuous culture in the world. The title of the book refers to how the Real People tribe describes Morgan, and non-Aborigines in general: mutants, the lot of 'em. In this mini-review, I'll share a few of the more noteworthy and unusual Real People customs. I must admit that some of the tribal ways described in the book rather appealed to me–except, perhaps, eating live worms.

First of all, as members of the tribe learn and develop new abilities throughout life, they change their names to reflect that. This really resonated with me because I always thought it was stupid to have to use the same name your whole life–one that you didn't even choose.

When one of them wants to change his or her name, the Real People don't have any of the cumbersome red tape that we have here. I'm reminded of the story of a certain man–we'll call him Joe–who brought all the paperwork for changing his name into the courtroom, only to have the judge go on a diatribe against name-changing. Finally the judge said, "What's your name, anyway?"

"Joe Shit," the man replied.

"Oh, okay," said the judge, slightly mollified. "Well, what do you want to change it to?"

"Frank Shit," said the man.

The Real People feel the purpose of the voice is for singing, celebrating and healing, not for mundane things like arguing about politics or ordering a pizza delivery. Therefore, they communicate via mental telepathy. Because everyone can read each other's minds, there's no lying or deceitful conduct. It saves a lot of wear and tear on the old vocal cords, plus, there's no dropped calls!

Music is considered medicine. Medicine is defined as *anything good that contributes to the welfare of the group.* There's no shlepping musical instruments around either. When they want to have a concert, natural materials are used to make percussion instruments, didgeridoos and bells, and of course there is always singing. "A musician carries the music within him. He needs no specific instrument. He is the music."

There is no written language, so songs are used to measure distance and time, and to record the history of the tribe. This is the meaning of *songlines*, a term you may have heard before. British writer Bruce Chatwin's 1987 book *The Songlines* documents his personal journey into the outback in order to research these ancient navigational paths.

A lot of my friends have birthdays this year, so let's cover the subject of birthday parties. Again I must agree with these Down Under folks. To them, celebration means something special has occurred. "There's nothing special about getting older–it just happens." Instead, celebrations take place "to acknowledge the person's talent, contribution to the community, personal and spiritual growth."

In the outback, there's no chocolate cake or banana splits. They eat whatever shows up that day and are very glad to receive it. If you're wondering about Christmas, there isn't one. In fact, there are no set holidays at all! (If we adopted that idea here, we'd eliminate the traffic jams and road rage caused by every single person in the tri-state area converging on the Merritt Parkway on Thanksgiving Day.)

The Real People's concept of land belonging to everyone is shared by most Native American tribes of the past (but just try to get your hands on a piece of Foxwoods or Mohegan Sun–you'll find yourself tossed out the teepee within ten beats of the tom

tom). This makes a lot of sense. How can someone own the Earth? The land wasn't made by a company and you can't take out a patent on it. And while we're on the subject, I've never understood how it can be against the law to own a plant [insert your favorite illegal botanical here].

The Real People don't say Grace at meals because they spend the whole day being grateful. They live to be 120 or 130, and when they're done with the planet and want to *return to forever,* they ask the spirits if it is for the highest good, then they call for a celebration of their life.

The following words are said to a tribe member at both the end and the beginning of life: "We love you and support you on the journey." Would someone please say that to me when I'm dying? After the party, the person goes into the desert, sits down in the sand, shuts down the body systems, and is gone in two minutes. The remains are food for wild animals and birds. No mess, no fuss.

Morgan's walkabout experience lasts for three months. When she emerges into civilization you can imagine how she looks. She wasn't into having her body cleansed by desert flies, as the natives did, so she doesn't smell too good either. Hence the less-than-enthusiastic reaction from the first people she meets upon stumbling out of the bush.

At this point she thinks, "Yesterday I had everything I needed: food, clothing, shelter, health care, companions, music, entertainment, support, a family, and lots of joyful laughter–all free . . . Today, unless I begged for money, I could not function. Everything required to exist had to be purchased . . . I was at this moment reduced to a filthy, tattered beggar . . . Only I knew the truth of the person contained within this exterior of poverty and grime."

If you've got eyes to try it sometime, just know that walkabouts ain't for sissies. Bon voyage. We love you and support you on your journey!

♪

THE MEANING IN ART

WE ARE BROADCASTING to ourselves a good part of our waking and sleeping hours. While awake, thoughts run through the mind continuously, giving opinions on what to observe and sense, and how to behave. Thoughts even comment on themselves, sometimes resulting in bizarre, circular arguments with oneself. Afterwards, we can lie down to rest from all that mental activity, but we can't hide from sleep's dreams.

Vacationing from the mind's workings can involve television, reading, sports and many other activities. Perhaps one's hobbies and pursuits are enjoyable not only for their own sake, but also because when one is focused on them the mind ceases its constant chatter. Or at least changes the subject.

Artists are fortunate in that they can process their obsessions through their art. This makes the obsession subservient to the artists' will. For example, fans of Salvador Dali will be familiar with the crutch that features prominently in many of his paintings. In his autobiography *The Secret Life of Salvador Dali* he relates how, as a child, he found the crutch while playing in the attic of his parents' house in Spain. "I immediately took possession of the crutch, and I felt that I should never again in my life be able to separate myself from it, such was the fetishistic fanaticism which seized me at the very first without my being able to explain it. The superb crutch! Already it appeared to me as the object possessing the height of authority and solemnity." After using the crutch in a few elaborately concocted rituals (he was a weird kid) it became for him a lifelong symbol of death and resurrection.

Music, visual art, dance, film, theater and poetry aren't about explaining anything. Actually, art does the opposite–it asks questions. Artists are explorers, of themselves and the universe. Artists and non-artists alike have opined on the purpose of Art, but maybe the best thing about making art is that it doesn't have to make sense.

The artist has a role in society. Art is not a pursuit undertaken to enhance one's personal lifestyle, even though Western cultures have anointed certain artists and made them celebrities. But the Cirque du Soleil acrobats or the Japanese Kodo drummers are nameless. They have achieved the pinnacle of artistic excellence in their fields, living for their art as much as any other artist, perhaps even more so—yet they are virtually anonymous.

Art provides nourishment to the creator as well as the receiver. Author Robert Fritz points out that creativity is about action. It's about envisioning (or otherwise inwardly sensing) something that doesn't yet exist that you would like to bring into being. The making of it is as important as the result.

The reason it's referred to as the *creative process* is that there are many stages along the way. If you're a chef, for instance— you imagine the dish, then chop, peel, marinate, make adjustments for disasters like the oven breaking, finally arranging the finished product on a plate for presentation to diners. In this case, the creation is eaten. Consumed. It undergoes a transformation and disappears from view, just like the Buddhist sand mandalas.

Environmental sculptor Andy Goldsworthy makes a living from disappearing art, though his art is not edible. He collects stones, driftwood, leaves, icicles and other natural materials, rearranging them in their habitat in extraordinary, ephemeral patterns. His creations melt, disperse, collapse. As the work disintegrates, we remember that all things share such a fate. "Things fall apart; the centre cannot hold . . ."

Marching toward entropy, if nothing is forever [except plutonium] then all we have are moments, one after the other. Music is played; its vibrations melt into the ears and the body. A dance is performed; the yang of the dancers is balanced by the yin of air molecules moving around in the space, propelled by the dancers' movements. The dance ends in stillness, as it began. The space between the dancers continues its own unseen orbit, its essence perhaps illuminated briefly by a well-angled spotlight.

While not a usually a performing art, literature unfolds in time for the reader. What is read exists afterward only in memory and feeling. Visual artworks of painting, sculpture, collage and photography may come closer to encapsulating meaning into a single moment. When I like a visual art piece, I usually stand gazing at it for awhile, which stretches the experience. (Beware: if you visit a gallery with artist friends, they will tour the whole show while you are still looking at painting number one! On a professional level, their involvement and understanding of the genre allows them to "get" a piece quickly, just as I can hear a few bars of music and know the essence of it without having to hear the whole thing. Life is short.)

We can also consider the so-called craft or folk arts like weaving, quilting or wood carving. When does a work cross the threshold of craft and enter the realm of art? Anything can join with Art–it just has to be "framed." There are so many differing ideas of what constitutes true art that it's not even worth arguing about.

Chalk it up to taste. To each his own. Tired platitudes–yet perhaps our understanding of art has been more colored by society than we thought. Maybe we've been trained to look at art only one way–the subjective way. The artist receives impressions that she or he filters through a painting, a composition, a dance. The artist renders the art, and the audience is affected by it according to their own personal associations brought up by the artwork.

But what if there is another kind of art–one that doesn't rely on subjective impressions? The legendary teacher and mystic G.I.Gurdjieff has declared there is, indeed, such art. *Objective art,* says Gurdjieff, contains an inherent meaning that is independent of the viewer's impressions. Its meaning is very specific and derives from a carefully calculated plan on the part of the artist.

In P. D. Ouspensky's book *In Search of the Miraculous* Gurdjieff says: "Imagine some scientific work–a book on astronomy or chemistry. It is impossible that one person should understand it in one way and another in another way. Everyone who is sufficiently prepared and who is able to read this book will understand what the author means, and precisely as the author means it. An objective work of art is just such a book, except that it affects the emotional and not only the intellectual side of man."

Ouspensky asks Gurdjieff if any works of objective art currently exist and receives this reply: "Of course they exist. The Great Sphinx in Egypt is such a work of art, as well as some historically known works of architecture, certain statues of gods, and many other things. There are figures of gods and of various mythological beings that can be read like books, only not with the mind but with the emotions, provided they are sufficiently developed. In the course of our travels in Central Asia we found, in the desert at the foot of the Hindu Kush, a strange figure which we thought at first was some ancient god or devil. At first it produced upon us simply the impression of being a curiosity. But after a while we began to feel that this figure contained many things, a big, complete, and complex system of cosmology. And slowly, step by step, we began to decipher this system. It was in the body of the figure, in its legs, in its arms, in its head, in its eyes, in its ears; everywhere. In the whole statue there was nothing accidental, nothing without meaning. And gradually we understood the aim of the people who built this statue. We began to feel their thoughts, their feelings . . . we grasped the meaning of what they wanted to convey to us across thousands of years, and not only the meaning, but all the feelings and the emotions connected with it as well. That indeed was art!"

If Mr. Gurdjieff and his companions had not taken the time to study the strange statue, they would not have heard its story. Despite technology and modern conveniences (or because of them) we have less and less time for creating and holding the inner space that art asks of us.

From the other room, the sublime sounds of Miles Davis playing "Blue in Green" walk in without knocking; legend has it someone once said to him, "I don't understand your music," to which Miles replied, "It took me twenty years of study and practice to work up to what I wanted to play in this performance. How can you expect to listen five minutes and understand it?"

Time is suspended
mind quiets, breathing deeply
my heart understands

♪

THE MYSTERY OF CORAL CASTLE

I VISITED A REMARKABLE attraction in Homestead, Florida. Coral Castle, a sculpture garden replicating a house, was built in the 1920s and 30s by one man using only hand tools. The man was Edward Leedskalnin, born in Latvia in 1887 to a family of stonemasons. Ed, as he is affectionately known by his many admirers, died in 1951 without ever revealing his procedure for extracting, moving and sculpting huge blocks of coral rock weighing many tons. Being five feet tall and a mere 120 lbs., it's doubtful that brute force would have been his preferred method.

Why did Ed build this incredible monument? The Coral Castle brochure would have you believe the massive undertaking was the result of unrequited love. All the publicity about Leedskalnin and Coral Castle hinges on this human interest angle. According to the promotional literature, after being spurned by his first love, nicknamed Sweet Sixteen, Ed built a "home" complete with furniture, made out of gigantic blocks of stone. Whether his motivation was to lure her back, to spite her, or to keep himself busy, we will never know. Maybe it was a combination of all three. In any case, the real fascination with Ed and his project lies not in warm and fuzzy love stories, but in the stone-cold fact of the monument itself.

When Ed died in 1951, a box was found on the property containing thirty-five hundred dollar bills. It was his life's savings, earned through the ten cent admission charge after he had opened the site to visitors. Sixty years later many thousands of them descend upon Coral Castle annually, drawn by the legend of the man who seemed to defy the laws of physics when he built this tribute to his Sweet Sixteen.

While the back story of Ed's lost love is a darn good yarn, it's unlikely that this chick who dumped him the day before the wedding was foremost in his mind while he was maneuvering sixty-ton rocks. When asked how he managed to manipulate the heavy stones, Ed would invariably reply that he understood the laws of weight and leverage. No further explanation was given–

unless one cares to pore over the writings on magnetism and electricity he left behind.

Amongst the stone carvings of Coral Castle are tables, two beds, rocking chairs, a sundial that is accurate to two minutes, and a massive stone gate that fits almost perfectly between two pillars and can be moved with one finger. Notably missing are items he certainly could have included if he had wanted: a stone television? A stone pool table? Rather, Ed seems to have spent his leisure time reading, and the various chairs are positioned to take advantage of the angles of the sun at different times of day.

Following in the tradition of Easter Island, the Egyptian pyramids and Stonehenge, Coral Castle has an air of mystery because nobody can say for sure how it was done. Ed worked at night by lantern light and allowed no observers.

I spent a few hours at the Castle. The stone chairs were incredibly comfortable. You had to wait your turn to sit in them because no one wanted to get up. The tour guide bandies about terms like "energy vortex," and there is, indeed, a calming energy permeating the space. Ed may have understood something of these more mystical energies, but as a self-taught engineer (he only made it to the 4th grade) his documented contributions in the field of electromagnetism have generated a great deal of interest amongst amateur scientists.

Leedskalnin's writings on electromagnetism are sold in the Coral Castle museum gift shop, as well as being available online from various websites. One of these is www.leedskalnin.com, where a collective of science geeks has devoted years to interpreting, extrapolating and experimenting based on Ed's cryptic writings.

The phenomenon of electricity is like a wild horse tamed and harnessed for our use. We can induce it and manipulate it, but we didn't invent it–Nature did. Originally electricity and magnetism were believed to be two distinct forces. Continuing in the direction outlined by Michael Faraday, in the early 1860s James Clerk Maxwell began publishing work showing that the interactions of positive and negative charges were controlled by one force, not two–hence the birth of the term "electromagnetism."

Physicists have explained that there are four fundamental forces in the universe: gravitational, electromagnetic, the strong nuclear force and the weak nuclear force. Of these, gravity is the weakest in the sense that it's the most easily overcome. One counteracts the gravitational pull of the earth simply by holding a pin or other metal object in the air with a magnet. (Or, as I like to do, you can just jump up and down.) Gravity can't be "cancelled out" because it only attracts. Electric forces, however, can attract and repel. It seems as if Ed Leedskalnin used both gravity and the electromagnetic force in constructing his manor of stone.

Curiously, many people prefer to ascribe feats of skill and precision (such as saxophone playing, for example) to mysterious, magical phenomena such as Teleportation, Alien Intervention, or Talent. In reality, all of the amazing skills I've heard or witnessed derive mainly from Intention, Focus, and Discipline. Any mystical powers that may come down the pike must be channeled by these Big 3 in order to be useable.

In recent years there have been other people besides Leedskalnin who decided to re-invent the wheel. One of these is Wally Wallington, a retired construction worker from Michigan. Wallington is a straightforward guy who didn't buy into the New Age frou-frou surrounding pop coverage of the pyramids and Stonehenge. Using "primitive" tools like the lever and the fulcrum, combined with gravity, Wallington accomplished feats worthy of the Discovery Channel and Ripley's Believe It Or Not–like moving a 10,000 lb. block 70 feet per hour, and relocating a 10 ton, 30x40 foot barn.

Since *homo sapiens* has been around for 200,000 years already, it doesn't seem feasible that we're only now coming around to effective construction methods, medical treatments, transportation, or food production. We know there were past civilizations of equal or greater stature than our own–so why is modern life held up as the pinnacle of human achievement? Moreover, the same things that have always been important to humans (food/water/shelter; relationships; meaningful work; meaningful play; faith in a higher power) have not changed. There's just more stuff around to distract us from them.

Today we live in the Culture of Technology. This culture is no different from any other in that it describes a creation myth that holds sway over its denizens. In this case, the myth is: Because of Technology Man Lives Better, Bigger, Brighter Than Before.

In order to validate this creation myth, technology must be produced and consumed at an ever-increasing pace. If production were to slow down–even for an instant–some people might wake up and want to trade in the myth for an older model. Yet the chief weapon of the Culture of Technology is simply, in the words of Morpheus in The Matrix, "most people are not ready to be unplugged."

♪

NOW WE ARE SIX, AGAIN

FOR SOME UNKNOWN REASON, one day I remarked to Gil, "Petra will be the first to go." This may end up to be true, though Providence has granted a reprieve. You see, our family of six consists of me, Gil, Harry and Zsa Zsa (the dogs), Marie and Petra (the cats).

Petra disappeared without a trace on a Wednesday. After a whole day and night,we gave up hope that she would come back, and suspected a coyote or a fisher cat got her. We began to eulogize her. (If you've never had pets, you're not expected to understand.) In tribute, a maudlin ballad would be most inappropriate, however–for over the course of several months we had witnessed a wondrous transfiguration of this marvelous creature.

First, a little background: Marie and Petra were litter sisters but they couldn't have been more different. Marie had always been the aloof type, because when you're a gorgeous calico life is easy. Petra was the sweet one, seemingly plain when she was young–grey with a cream colored belly. Before she matured into her eventual three colors of grey and cream with a rust undercoat (cats with more than two colors are always female) we thought she was a boy. Petra's original name, therefore, was Pierre. The two of them were named after Marie and Pierre Curie. I'll never forget the Brooklyn vet's comment: "Well, Pierre's a girl. Do you want to change her name, *or what?*" Not that I'm married to gender-specific names, but since my last female cat was named Raul (not my choice; I saved her from a tortuous life in a frat house when I was in college) I decided to go with a more traditional route this time around.

The name Petra, in addition to being a feminized form of Pierre, was also the name of a character in my favorite musical–*A Little Night Music* by Stephen Sondheim. Of tangential interest is that the character of Petra in this musical was at one point played by the actress Susan Terry. I never met Ms. Terry, but when I lived in Manhattan I used to get her mail occasionally. (No checks though.) The synchronicity of this is based on the fact that I didn't know she had played Petra in *A Little Night Music* until many years after my own Petra was born.

Petra was always very affectionate, albeit mischievous. And her coat was soft, not like Marie's which was coarse . Marie and Petra shared a propensity for avoirdupois that saw them both hit eighteen pounds, so I thought of them as my guard cats.

At one point Petra began losing weight. She also developed a pink, wrinkled growth on her back that became as big as a grape. When I brought her to the vet for this, he said it would cause her more stress to remove it than to leave it alone. One day, however, I noticed that the growth was completely gone. Petra had licked it off all by herself, and it never came back.

We were still concerned about her health, being that she was really slimming down without having signed up for Jenny Craig or working out with any aerobics videos. She had taken to running around outside at our Pennsylvania place, but we couldn't believe that mere physical activity was responsible. She also vomited a lot, which worried us somewhat even though it's a common thing with cats.

After an extended stay in Pennsylvania, surrounded by nature, Petra began to spend more time outside than in. She roamed all over the property, and we would often see her bounding across the grass. Always a fan of toy mice, she began to hunt, and sometimes capture, small game. At 15 years old, Miss Petra had transformed herself from a couch cat to a strong and wily hunter, a lithe and elegant enchantress. She stopped vomiting. (She still scratched the furniture though.)

When she was outside, she wanted nothing to do with us. It was as if we intruded on her outdoor experience. Then, two days before she disappeared, she started coming up to be petted when she saw us outside. On Wednesday we were out on the deck with the camera. "Oh, look at Petra" Gil said. (We were always saying that.) She was lolling around the bottom of the stairs, stretching out and rolling over on her back. She was so beautiful. We took her picture. That was the night she didn't come home.

The previous day, I had been talking with my student Ed about "playing the rests." I was explaining that the rests are not just the "notes of silence" that we had been taught as kids; the rests actually have a "sound" that manifests as weight as opposed to vibration. True story: When my brother and I were kids, our parents took us to Colonial Williamsburg on a family trip. We entered one of the buildings and all of a sudden my brother and I yelled in pain and grabbed our heads! We didn't know what was happening–we felt a tremendous pressure like the world's most super headache.

"Oh, they must be hearing the burglar alarm," said the guide. As soon as he said the words "burglar alarm" I suddenly heard the very high pitched sound that was supposedly beyond the range of human hearing. Obviously we left that particular building pretty quickly. Later in life, there were a few other places I could never go: backstage at Hartford's West India Club; the gem exhibit at the Natural History Museum; a television store on Broadway near my old place in Washington Heights.

The experience of hearing–or more accurately, feeling–those burglar alarms taught me that sound exerts pressure even though it's silent. If you've ever been on top of a mountain, you can feel the opposite kind of silence–the kind that is below the range of human hearing. It's ponderous and solemn. This is the weight that musical rests have.

As Thursday progressed and we felt that Petra was not coming back, the weight of her absence rested amongst us like a mountaintop. All the animals were subdued; Marie in particular just laid in one spot then another, and wouldn't eat. Our gaze kept wandering toward the driveway, the woods, the rocks behind the house, in the mad hope of seeing our dear kitty returning after all. A sudden thundershower suggested that her small skeleton was being washed away somewhere, and maybe someday someone would find her orange collar with its little round tag. Night came. We barely slept.

The next day, I got up and went to take the dogs out. A howl from behind the basement door broke the morning stillness; I rushed to the door, and a ravenous Petra bounded out, heading directly for her food dish! I screamed and cried, shouting unintelligibly to Gil, "Petra's home!" We spent the remainder of Friday in a gentle state of shock mixed with relief. I went on the Internet and ordered a radio collar transmitter and receiver set. Petra got an extra helping of wet food, and lots of hugs and kisses.

Telling this story to an acquaintance named Linda, she said something similar had happened to her. Dressed to go to a Christmas party, she got in her car and went to pick up the babysitter. On the side of the road, there was her cat Schwartz–dead. *I can't deal with this*, thought Linda. She kept driving. The momentum of the evening's plans somehow guided her through. She went to the party and came home exhausted. Upon arising, Linda went out to retrieve poor Schwartz's body. She opened the garage door, and out walked Schwartz!

These kinds of stories certainly give credence to the folk legend of cats having nine lives. Even more interesting though, at least to me, was observing my reactions and behaviors during the whole feline fiasco. For instance, even though a part of me did not believe Petra was dead (Denial? Clairvoyance?), I watched another part of myself as it went through the grieving process. When she was literally resurrected (from the basement!) I watched myself go into hysterics, even though I could have controlled myself if I'd wanted to. I thought of the women who wail at the graveside of a loved one; culturally this is not in my background at all, but it definitely felt good to release the emotion. As Monty Python says: "It's better than bottlin' it up, ennit?"

Long live Petra, and Schwartz–may their tails forever wave!

EPILOGUE

Petra was not the first to go. Zsa Zsa died on Aug. 1, 2012 of congestive heart failure. She was followed by Harry in 2013. My mother died shortly after Harry, then Marie left us in 2014. My husband Gil died in March of 2015. Petra dropped dead right in front of me as I was getting ready to go to work in July of that same year.

♪

ON A CLEAR DAY, IN E FLAT

WE OFTEN DESCRIBE innovators and leaders throughout history as "ahead of their time." This phrase is nowhere more apt than in the field of medicine, whose pioneers are usually derided and scorned for their efforts. Potential detractors hide amongst colleagues like wolves in sheep's clothing. If one feels his or her reputation about to be dented by the innovations of another, a battle may break out, because scientists tend to value their reputations above all. A good reputation is the hard-earned result of years of research and practical applications in one's specialty, and is the pathway to obtaining the funds necessary for further research and development. In Science, rebuilding a damaged reputation takes decades, unlike in the Arts or even in Politics. (Indeed, the interval between a politician's fall and subsequent rehabilitation seems to get shorter by the week.)

While the lay public imagines that scientists are all day thinking outside of the box, the reality is quite different. As in other fields, medical academies suffer from the notorious That's The Way We've Always Done Things Around Here Syndrome, and many innovations take far longer than necessary to be developed and offered to patients.

It is a flawed system, but perhaps a necessary one—charlatans do exist, after all, and *caveat emptor* is as timely a slogan now as when it was first uttered by Julius Caesar or whoever a couple of thousand years ago. (Not for nothing: if the Food and Drug Administration is the gatekeeper du jour, a citizen can only hope that an equally stringent and draconian approval process might someday be adopted for the concoctions of the Finance Industry. While we're young.) That said, a quick look through the ever-expanding Whistleblower's Tales of Big Pharma reveals the sad truth that deception occurs on both sides.

While visiting my ophthalmologist we got to talking about Ignaz Semmelweis. In case you've never heard of him, you may pay homage the next time you go in a public washroom and see the sign *Employees Must Wash Hands*. Back in the 19th century when no one knew what germs were, Semmelweis made the medical students in his teaching hospital wash their hands before entering the maternity ward, where the rate of death from infection sometimes reached 30%. Previously, students had gone directly from the cadaver room to the maternity room without a second thought.

When the death rate plunged to less than 2% thanks to his new policy, Semmelweis was fired. Stunned, but still passionate about his discovery, Dr. Semmelweis went from Vienna back to his native Hungary. Despite his success in virtually eliminating childbed fever in his maternity ward in Pest, hand washing was again rejected by his colleagues outside the hospital. Ridiculed for daring to suggest the existence of something we now call "bacteria," the good doctor's mental health suffered, and he spent his last days in a lunatic asylum.

My ophthalmologist began to tell me another made-for-Hollywood story about his late colleague Dr. Charles Kelman (1930-2004) who reigns as a veritable deity in the Ophthalmological Hall of Fame. But it was not always so.

Kelman grew up in Forest Hills, Queens, during the big band era. He was the son of hard-working Jewish immigrant parents who paid for his music lessons; little Charlie's dream was to be on stage performing, like his heroes Benny Goodman and Artie Shaw. Charlie's father said, "You can be anything you want to be–a singer, a saxophone player, but first–be a doctor."

Kelman was not a brilliant student, but he got into Tufts and plodded along academically, devoting most of his time and attention to his music career. When his father was diagnosed with cancer, however, Kelman was knocked into overdrive. He buckled down to his studies and graduated in two years, going on to medical school to study ophthalmology. Sadly, Kelman *père* died six months before the son received his diploma.

The same drive that had characterized his dreams of stardom now fed the young Dr. Kelman's medical ambitions. He became fascinated with the study of the eye, inventing a device that he felt would revolutionize cataract surgery. Unused to the professional rivalries in his new calling, however, he was shocked to see his invention stolen from under him by one of his mentors.

Crushed, but not given to giving up, Kelman undertook research for a new invention. He was bent on modernizing the antiquated method of cataract surgery that required several weeks of recovery time for patients, and necessitated the wearing of thick glasses after the operation.

Meanwhile, the young doctor still pursued his music. He wrote songs constantly, pitching them to stars like Frankie Avalon and Fabian. While pitching a song to the head of Chancellor Records one day, he was signed himself! Using the pseudonym Kerry Adams in order to avoid criticism from his medical colleagues, he was on the way to stardom when Chubby Checker arrived on the scene and the music of the 60s began yet another transformation. Kelman's ambitions were smashed, again.

Obsessed with fame and determined to have it, Kelman embarked on research to invent another new surgical procedure, but this time in secret. Working with only a couple of devoted nurse-assistants, he spent three years developing a machine that would allow the extraction of the lens of the eye through a small incision, unlike the 180 degree incision which was the protocol of the time. Just when his grant money was running out, he had a Eureka moment while getting his teeth cleaned at the dentist. The new tool that his dentist proudly showed off to him was just the thing for breaking up a cataract and removing the lens!

Intrigue followed Kelman at every step, in constant dialogue with his paranoia. His rightful prize of fame and fortune had eluded him twice already, and he would not allow it to be taken away again. He put all his efforts into adapting the new device, conducting trials on cat eyes. He had no home life anymore, and his wife left him. Kelman then did the unthinkable: he formed a partnership with the manufacturer of his device, the *phacoemulsifier*.

Doctors were not supposed to go into business with industry. The ophthalmological community took revenge. The well-trod narrative of Renegade Inventor vs. The Establishment played out once more, with feeling. But word spread; doctors heard about the new type of cataract surgery and came to New York to learn it from Dr. Kelman himself. Combining his musical and medical careers at last, after the seminars Kelman put on stage shows complete with big bands and dancers for the visiting doctors.

Despite winning more and more converts to the new cataract procedure, however, Kelman continued to face threats from the American Academy of Ophthalmology. Realizing that the Academy's less-than-enthusiastic reception to phacoemulsification would haunt him for years to come and perhaps ruin his career, he decided to go over their heads. His credentials in medicine and in the music world got him booked on television! What to the wondering eyes of the Academy of Ophthalmology board should appear, on Feb. 21, 1975 shortly after 11:30 p.m., but Charles Kelman, M.D. as Johnny Carson's guest on *The Tonight Show*.

After his *Tonight Show* appearance, Kelman's private practice took off. He continued to create new ophthalmological procedures, and married again. He wrote books and articles, and was invited on other talk shows like Merv Griffin and David Letterman where he discussed his new autobiography *Through My Eyes*. One interviewer was curious about Kelman's double life as doctor and entertainer. He asked, "if you had to pick one, which one would you choose?" Kelman responded, "There are basic needs in life–clothing, shelter, food, love–but there's a need I don't think is recognized, and that's the need, for many people, to do something else. And very often they go back to one of their childhood dreams."

Dr. Kelman continued to perform at medical events and fundraisers, Atlantic City casinos, and he even rented Carnegie Hall to do a show. The recipient of dozens of awards for his contributions to medicine, he was finally lauded by his former nemesis, the American Academy of Ophthalmology, with their highest honor: the 2003 Laureate Award. He died six months later at the age of 74.

Today phacoemulsification is the most commonly performed surgical procedure in the developed world. Almost 10 million people per year regain their vision through devices and techniques created by Dr. Charles Kelman. Additionally, Kelman has been called the "grandfather of all small incision surgery" because his innovation enabled vast improvements in operations on the gall bladder, brain, and spinal cord.

A one-hour film about his life was made by PBS station WLIW. In the film Kelman is shown doing his stage act–cute and a little corny, but compelling nonetheless. In the finale, he remarks:

"If there's any message in this, maybe it's that you should go out and do your own thing–whatever it is– and give in to that secret dream inside you."

Sometimes it takes two dreams to tango.

♪

OPEN LETTER TO GREYSON CHANCE

DEAR GREYSON,

Even though it was only a few days ago, I can't remember just how your video made its way onto my computer. You see, so much has happened since then: Hundreds if not thousands of other singers have uploaded their videos to YouTube; thousands if not millions of cars, buses and aircraft have roared to their respective codas; and trillions of birds, reptiles and insects have filled the forests with their songs. Plus, I had a lot of laundry to do.

You're 12 years old, so you've probably studied the properties of sound in school. Since sound is vibration, that means every sound we make when we play music creates vibrations that extend into the world through the medium of air (unless we're playing underwater). They probably go out to the whole universe–because when you think about it, where does the earth end and the sky begin?

The songs of the forest creatures serve various purposes that are essential for their well-being and indeed, their very survival. When an airplane flies over the forest, it disrupts the songs of the frogs, crickets, birds and other creatures who live there. Then they have to start their songs over again, before they even get to the bridge!

Likewise, the music we play has an effect not only on our immediate surroundings but also beyond that. Vibrations can travel a long way even when the sound is no longer audible. When they hit something solid, they cause the object itself to vibrate as the waves are absorbed.

When I was in music school, I had a friend named Tom who was an art school student. He also loved music, and he played drums, so he was always hanging out with us musicians. Tom was deaf. The way he listened, and the way he played, was by feeling sound vibrations. We music school students thought it was pretty amazing. But we also thought, he could never be a REAL musician because he can't hear. Looking back on those days, I wish I had paid more attention to the ways that Tom must have experienced music. Now, after I've been a musician for more than 40 years, I am just beginning to understand that music is so much more than most of us think.

Buckminster Fuller is said to have remarked that 99% of what is real cannot be seen or touched. We can't see or touch music–but it's real, right? What makes it real are its invisible vibrations. They can't be touched, but they certainly can be felt!

Getting back to you, Greyson. When you sang you told me a lot of things. You told me the emotion of love is the most powerful energy there is, and that we could influence the whole world with it. You also said purity of intent is really important. Without that, it's pointless, right? (Because I enjoyed your singing so much, I'm just writing down what you said in case you forget it when you're older. That happens, you know.) Also, we say a lot without using words. We say a lot without even being consciously aware of it.

You seem like a pretty together dude; I may be a lot older and more experienced than you, but sometimes age is irrelevant. Only the body ages; the spirit is timeless. Your spirit shines through in your song about the wife who dies from cancer and her husband follows her, reminding me of the myth of Orpheus and Eurydice. You have an unusual sensitivity, and a capacity for making highly personal emotions accessible. You can make lots of people listen to you. What a gift!

Of course, our gifts are not given just for the enhancement of our personal lifestyle. With these gifts comes tremendous responsibility. One is a role model, whether one likes it or not. Our fans look up to us for leadership, in a way. They'd like us to show the qualities of grace, excellence, service, humility–not only on stage but also in our personal lives–so that they can see those abstract elements personified and strive to embody them in their own lives.

We are disappointed when our heroes do not live up to their image, position, or office. Recent falls from grace by Tiger Woods, Eliot Spitzer, Amy Winehouse (1983-2011) come to mind. Yet we are all human, and all capable of falling. Sometimes we feel far away from the ideals we seem to display to others, or we feel smothered by those ideals. As the lonely path winds upward toward the mountain peak, it gets narrower and narrower, and harder to stay on.

When one lives in the public eye, it's actually a good idea to pull back occasionally. Many of our modern era geniuses—performers like Frank Sinatra and Miles Davis, for example, went through periods of seclusion after which they had a comeback. One could say they did not plan those inactive periods—that surely they would have preferred to continue their careers without abatement. And yet, isn't there a deeply hidden aspect of spirit that knows when one must retreat? To re-group. To re-align all aspects of Self, so the work can continue. So one can continue to serve.

We also know that many of the truly profound among us are not famous at all. Being famous and maintaining that fame takes a lot of time and energy (not to mention money), and frequently sages shy from public life in order to lead a more contemplative existence. This creates a space from which they can develop themselves, and thus be of more service to their communities.

Others, like you, have a gift for widespread communication—a perilous, albeit important, path. Navigating the public waters exposes one to the whole world's negative elements. They are attracted to the light and they swarm around you. You've been famous for a week and a half already so I'm sure you've noticed this.

Lady Gaga gave you some really good advice when she said to stay away from girls. She didn't mean that literally; she was expressing the idea of keeping one's own counsel so as not to get distracted by unimportant matters. There's only so much time in the day, and you have only written two songs, so you need to write some more. Write every day, even if it's only for a few minutes—I know you have a lot of homework. Otherwise people in the business will use you to sing other people's songs and not your own. They will try to make you send out their own messages, instead of the ones your spirit is hearing. (I'm no seer, by the way—all the images in my crystal ball were previously recorded.)

So many songs to write, so little time. Should I write a symphony, or a string quartet, or a song about a dream I had last night? Composers know that it's best to write for the groups you can get to play your music. You belong to the school choir. It would be awesome if you wrote some pieces for them. The human voice is a beautiful instrument.

Have you heard of Cole Porter? Billie Holiday? Glenn Gould? Speaking of Gould, I'll bet you would really dig listening to the two versions of Bach's Goldberg Variations he recorded. The first version was made when he was a young man. The second version was made just a few months before he died at age 50. Check them out.

Songs written over three hundred years ago are still being performed, so the energy put into motion by those songs is still out there, making the world a better place. We composers hope our songs will still be played 300 years from now, even if it's too late to collect royalties. In fact, it would be interesting if all composers would refrain from composing anything they felt was not worthy of lasting 300 years. Do you think that could ever happen? Well, at least you and I can do our part.

Your friend in music,

Su Terry

♪

THE PERU CHRONICLES

JFK Airport, New York City, Dec. 2, 2009.

SCHEDULED TO TAKE a LAN Airlines red eye to Lima, I arrive at JFK around 8:30 p.m. and position myself at the end of the longest check-in line I've ever seen.

GOOD: a LAN agent pulls me and another passenger out of the queue and escorts us directly to the check-in counter! I still don't know why, unless it was due to racial profiling (*Hey Juanita, go pull out those two gringos before they start bitching and moaning about the wait.*) BAD: At the check-in counter the agent says to me, "You're not scheduled to depart until tomorrow night." Egad! My mind quickly reviews the online booking process. I concede to myself that in ditzing around trying to get the cheapest fare, it was possible I might have confirmed the wrong flight. GOOD: I had bought the travel insurance. BAD: I doubted that it covered bonehead mistakes like booking one's flight for the wrong day. GOOD: The agent is really nice. His name is Nelson. He gives me the LAN Reservations phone number and tells me to call them and have them change it. BAD: I keep getting disconnected.

Then the brilliant idea comes to me that I could just buy a one-way ticket to Lima and straighten it out with Travelocity later. After all, I have insurance, right? So I leave my luggage by the check-in counter and trot across the room to the ticket kiosk. "Oh yes, we do have a seat available for this flight" (GOOD!) says the lady. "That will be $1,746.00 please. Cash or charge?" Considering I had paid $700 for the entire 3-leg flight, this was BAAAAAAAD.

Many phone calls ensue. Meanwhile, the check-in line is dwindling down to a precious few. I review all the possibilities–throw caution to the wind and buy the one-way ticket, hoping the insurance I had bought would cover it. Or should I go back home (another $50 cab ride) and come back the next night, and in the meantime try to change my connecting flight, cancel my hotel room in Cusco, and go directly to Pisac from the Cusco airport?

"But I'm already at JFK!" my Inner Whiner intoned. If there's anything she hates, it's retracing her steps.

Oh look, there's no one left in the check-in line. My luggage is still sitting over there. "Check-in is about to close," says the LAN lady helpfully. "Do you want the one way ticket?"

A dialogue ensues between the angel over my right shoulder, and the devil over my left. The devil says: "Wouldn't you like to think of yourself as a person who can throw down 1700 smackers on a plane ticket if you're in a jam? Aren't you capable of that? C'mon, you'll get it back. Don't ruin your trip. What are you, chicken?"

The angel says: "Dear, I'm sure someday you'll be a person who can drop $1700 on one third of a ticket that costs half of that. But right now, you're not. Be sensible."

Suddenly, as if from above, a peace descends upon me. I accept my fate. I walk back to Nelson the check-in guy and say, "Are you working tomorrow? I'll see you then." He looks at me intently and says, "You really need to fly tonight, don't you?" Without waiting for an answer, he begins typing furiously on his computer. He picks up the phone and calls his supervisor. He hangs up, points to me and says, "You're flying tonight!" GOOOOOOOOOOOD!

The devil then chimes in with a worried tone: "Wait a minute. What if this happened for a reason? What if you weren't supposed to take this flight? What if this plane is going to crash!" BAD!

Then the angel: "My my, why all the confusion? That was just those silly Fates playing with your head, giving you a lesson in Acceptance. You know how they like to joke around." The angel's wisdom rang true. I realized that as soon as I had given up my plans, accepting the fact that I would have to go back home, adjust my travel arrangements, fork over an extra $100 in cab fares–this was the point that I got on the flight after all.

The plane did not crash, although there was a sick passenger right behind me, and for a while there it seemed as if we might have to land prematurely. Somehow she recovered. Another catastrophe averted. The only thing lost was a night's sleep–and that passenger's dinner.

Landing in Cusco, Peru at 11 a.m., I only had 24 hours to spend and I made the most of it. Walked all around, even in the rain. At night, all the Americans were going to Jack's Cafe on Choquechaca St. so I didn't go there. Instead I had dinner and sat in with some Peruvian musicians at a club called La Normandie, down the street from my hotel. They were doing a strange mix of 70s pop and traditional Peruvian songs. The drummer did not have a drum set. He played a traditional Latino instrument called a *cajon*, which means "box." It is a box. He made it sound like a whole kit! The sax player, a young man named Luiz, had only been playing for six years. He wanted to take lessons with me but I was leaving the next day. I sent him a copy of my book *Practice Like The Pros* as a consolation though.

In the morning, I scouted around some more and found a luthier's shop on one of the side streets. The luthier's name was Sabino, and he had some beautiful stringed instruments as well as some traditional Peruvian flutes called *quenas*. I tried one of his guitars and a *quena*, but I didn't buy anything as I was still early into my trip.

I returned to the Rumi Punku Hotel in preparation for the next phase of my journey. In the lobby I met the first of my traveling companions with whom I would soon be sharing a series of esoteric and insightful experiences: the handsome Patrick, and the magical Canadians, Heather and Edsel. At noon, shaman Diego arrived with his own car plus a taxi with driver to transport us and our luggage to Pisac, our headquarters for the extraordinary week which was to follow.

The ancient Inca village of Pisac was 30 kilometers away. We were to spend a week at Melissa-Wasi, a compound of private homes reserved for our use. The compound lies in a beautiful valley surrounded on all sides by *apus*—spirits of the sacred mountains that have served as sentinels of this valley for many centuries. The magic of the ancient Inca Empire still seems to exist here–one feels it in the silence.

At one time the Inca civilization ruled the vast and majestic Andes Mountain Range. Though it lasted fewer than one hundred years (1438-1532) it was the largest empire on Earth at the time, encompassing Colombia, Ecuador, Peru, Bolivia, Chile, and northern Argentina. The remarkable terraced farming on the mountains is a tradition that remains throughout Peru today.

The Quechua language is still spoken here, along with Spanish which was brought by the Conquistadors in the 16th century. Expecting a backward civilization, Pizarro and his army were shocked by the wealth and sophistication of the indigenous people. Sadly but not surprisingly, the Conquistadors destroyed both the Inca architectural wonders and the finely wrought religious and art objects of gold and silver they found there.

Arriving at Melissa-Wasi we met the rest of our group for the first time: Robin, Helene, Harold, Irene, Cindy, Merav, and the two Daves. Our thirteenth member, Daragh–a young Irishman currently living in Cusco–would join us later. We were briefed on the house rules by Milagros. As the partner of shaman Diego, she was a vital part of the success of our trip. She cooked and cleaned (aided by three very sweet assistants), managed the extremely active life of her 5-year-old son, and looked after us during the ceremonies.

What ARE these ceremonies of which I speak? What kind of a trip was this, anyway? To casual acquaintances I described my trip as a "spiritual journey," but it was much more. The purpose of this trip–the reason why people from all over the globe come here– was to experience the insights and healing received from ingesting a plant medicine called *Ayahuasca*.

Ayahuasca is made by boiling equal parts of a vine and a leafy plant native to South America. The resulting brew is a dark brown, bitter concoction better chugged than sipped. This was to be the second Ayahuasca series for me, and I couldn't wait to drink the stuff again. After having taken the medicine in Ecuador several months earlier, I realized it had much more to offer than what I was able to assimilate in my first "journeys," as the Ayahuasca experiences are known.

Preparation for the journeys involves a strict diet, periods of fasting, abstention from sexual activity, and silent contemplation or prayer, for *Madre* Ayahuasca gives tough love. She also demands your complete attention, and your complete surrender to her power.

One experiences many things on an Ayahuasca journey. Often the first sensation will be the urge to vomit, hence the

TERRY

preponderance of plastic buckets amongst the temple decor. In ceremony parlance this is known as *purging*, and it rids one's body of toxins. Since the urge to purge may come on very quickly, one always has one's bucket within reach–especially since the ceremonies are held in the dark.

In the darkness one has many visions, although they are not like hallucinations. You know they are only visions and you can go outside if they become too overwhelming. The types of visions vary widely. You may be shown episodes from your life that you had forgotten. You may be visited by spirits, entities, creatures of all sorts. You may see parts of your body disappear, or be ushered into strange realms of unfamiliar beings and structures. One can ask for, and receive, information about virtually anything–the plant world, the animal world, the body, mind or spirit. And you will certainly be shown truths about yourself that your conscious mind may have been hiding from, or ignoring.

Moments of ecstasy and perfect peace will be balanced out by moments of terror and profound sadness–if not on this journey, then on the next. Surrendering your will to that of the medicine is absolutely essential. Whatever happens, you just have to accept it and not try to fight it. Resistance is futile! In short, taking Aya is no picnic.

Mother Aya seems to give each person what he or she needs at the time. A journey lasts several hours. The ceremony starts at 8 or 9 p.m. and closes at 2 or 3 a.m. At certain points, the shaman offers additional doses of the medicine to anyone who feels they need more.

I was particularly struck by how the perception of time is altered during a journey. Each moment is so full that by the time the ceremony ends, you're pretty whipped. Why would anybody want to do this, you may ask. Believe me, there were times during the journey that I asked myself the same thing. But then I would learn something extraordinary, and I'd remember.

The shaman who leads the ceremony is responsible for guiding the collective energy in the room, and his or her skill in doing so will have a great deal to do with your personal experience. During the ceremony the shaman sings *icaros*, medicine songs. When you're in the middle of a strange and disturbing part of your journey, the songs seem to float by like a lifeline, grabbing the attention and calming the spirit so one can continue to open one's heart to *Madre* Ayahuasca. Through this act of simple surrender, one is able to learn the true meaning of Love and Compassion—mere words, unless they are truly felt by the heart. This is the Love of which we've heard spoken, but in our modern life sometimes seems very far away.

The people who journey with you will become part of your tribe. The bonds that form during this intense week are evident in the videos and photos posted online. I dedicate these Chronicles to my tribe. It is a big tribe, probably much bigger than we realize—and we welcome those who walk with us on the seeker's path.

♪

REALITY

IN THE 1980s I became aware of a little known literary genre colloquially termed The Seth Books, and more formally known as The Seth Material. The books contain transcripts and details of trance sessions held by a medium named Jane Roberts (and recorded by her husband Robert Butts) channeling an entity named Seth. Seth comments on many aspects of human existence, but the gist of his message is this: you create your own reality. Boom. That's it.

One then asks, does that mean that whatever happens to me, I myself am responsible for it? Holy smoke. When one envisions all the possible scenarios of illness, mutilation, death and ruin of all sorts (which we often seem to prefer over visions of health, wealth and happiness) one is tempted to think how unfair and blame the victim-ish such a philosophy is. Yet when we use our 20-20 hindsight, it's easier to see how our own interpretations of reality may have induced various events in our lives to come about.

Seth is not, of course, the only one who ever spoke about the idea of creating your own reality. It's an idea that gets repackaged continuously, most recently, perhaps, with the ubiquitous DVD and book *The Secret*. When my friend Elizabeth gave me a copy of the DVD a couple of years ago I was amazed at the film's high production qualities. It was like a Hollywood blockbuster! Being a student of esoteric philosophy since the 1970s, I was accustomed to hissy cassette tapes and dog-eared paperbacks–because back then, content was king. Like jazz musicians listening rapturously to scratchy old recordings from the likes of Clifford Brown or Bud Powell, if you were into this stuff before there was "New Age," then you don't need Dolby Surround Sound and Imax 3D to appreciate it.

The Secret is all about the Law of Attraction, which is just another way of saying–guess what–you create your own reality. There are countless sources of information on this topic, but most fail to mention one of the requirements necessary for actually understanding the concept. That requirement is merely this: one must quiet one's mind to make space for new ideas.

Could it be that there is no objective reality separate from the individual mini-realities that each one of us creates for him/herself? Robert Anton Wilson, the iconoclastic philosopher and author, assures us there is no objective reality–but I'm still not sure! What if there really is an objective reality, but the human mind is unable to perceive or comprehend the objective reality in its entirety? After all, most of us can only imagine three or four dimensions and we're done. Seeing as how physicists are saying there are at least 26 dimensions, that would mean our understanding is only a fraction of what's really out there.

In the 70s, I studied a little Kabbalah on my own. I had tried to study with a Rabbi who was on the campus of my university, but he wouldn't teach me anything about it. At the time I thought it was because I was a woman and that ticked me off. Looking back, I can see it was my own thinking that caused me to view his reluctance that way. Who knows what the Rabbi's actual reason was?

The main thing I got from my studies was this: The Kabbalistic writings say that the magnificence and the vastness of God is so powerful that we humans aren't capable of taking it all in–that it would destroy us! This idea also appears in the Ancient Greek legend of Icarus: he tried to escape Crete, where the king was holding him prisoner, by flying away on giant wings bound with wax. But he flew too close to the sun and his wings melted. So might we, too, have a meltdown if we get too much of a dose of reality at one time. Perhaps another moral from the myth of Icarus is that we can't just fly away from our problems by slapping on a pair of wings–whether they be of feathers or some other folly .

The Russian author P. D. Ouspensky puts yet another twist in ye olde reality pretzel with his short novel *The Strange Life of Ivan Osokin*. In the novel Osokin meets a magician who grants him the ability to relive his life. Osokin expects that awareness of his future will enable him to avoid all the mistakes he had made in the past. He soon finds out that his choices are still nothing more than mechanical reactions, making change extremely difficult.

There is a scene from the film *Avatar* where the main character is told that the tribe cannot give any knowledge to the *dream walkers* because "their cup is already full." This is a reference to the treasured Buddhist tale of the Master who keeps filling the student's teacup till it overflows, commenting that the student's mind is just like the teacup.

The parable gives a clear image of how one must empty oneself of old beliefs before one can receive new ones. We can learn about other possibilities by reading a book or watching a movie–yet these are things outside ourselves, and ultimately our cup will overflow unless we empty it first.

As we march through life creating our own realities, there are so many choices that sometimes one longs for the best one to just jump out and declare itself. The 60s gave us the wonderful expression "go with the flow." But here's the thing: you have to know where the flow is before you can go with it.

♪

THE RINGING CEDARS SERIES

I ARRIVED IN VILCABAMBA, Ecuador after an exhausting all-day journey originating in Pisac, Peru. My friends Brian and Meredith, assisted by our friend Julia, had dinner waiting for me. Their beautiful lodge was illuminated by candlelight for the nightly two-hour electricity blackout–a conservation effort in effect over the entire country.

Was it the candlelight, the company, the altitude, hunger, or the crazy week I'd had in Peru that put me in a particularly receptive state of mind? For whatever reason, something Julia mentioned at dinner stuck in my mind for months afterward.

We had been discussing the workshop I would be conducting that weekend on the Six Healing Sounds, a branch of Chinese Qi Gong in which sound vibrations are used to eliminate blockages in the physical body and the energy body. The idea of "healing sounds" reminded Julia of a book she had read called *Anastasia.* She began to tell us about it.

The book opens by discussing a certain type of cedar tree that grows in Siberia. Sometimes, after one of these trees attains the age of about five hundred years, it begins to emit a ringing sound. Inhabitants of this remote area of Russia know that the ringing is a signal for the tree to be cut down and its wood distributed (for free) to good-hearted people, in order to heal any diseases and malaise they may have.

Vladimir, the narrator, is captain of a ship that plies the rivers of that region. Two elderly Siberians ask him if he will bring some men and equipment to cut down a ringing cedar in their forest. Thus begins the remarkable relationship between Vladimir and the elders' granddaughter–a young enchantress named Anastasia who lives alone in a forest glade and possesses seemingly superhuman knowledge and abilities.

After spending three days in the glade with her, Vladimir wishes to bring Anastasia to "civilization" so that she may teach others how to attain these abilities. Anastasia, however, has a better idea. She remains in the forest in the Siberian taiga and entrusts Vladimir with the task of writing a book about her. Nine books later the series has been translated to twenty languages and over 10 million copies have been sold.

Keep in mind that the Ringing Cedars Series is purported to be a work of nonfiction. In this respect it reminds one of Carlos Castaneda's body of work. When Castaneda wrote about his experiences with the Yaqui Indian sorcerer Don Juan, there was a great deal of controversy over whether the works were indeed nonfiction as Castaneda claimed. (His third book, in fact, was used as his Ph.D thesis for his anthropology degree at UCLA.) Yet devotees of his work are completely unconcerned with the veracity issue, citing the teachings themselves, and not the characters or events depicted, as the crux of Castaneda's contribution.

Similarly, the issue of whether or not Anastasia truly exists is not the point of the Ringing Cedars Series (also known as the "Anastasia books"). The point is to convey a set of teachings which, taken individually, can also be found in the documented history of a wide variety of esoteric traditions. Just as the popular book and video *The Secret* is basically a repackaging of ideas relating to the ancient metaphysical concept of the Law of Attraction and its subsequent development by Esther and Jerry Hicks and others, the Anastasia books don't have a great deal of exclusive content in terms of the ideas presented. But their scope is so vast that even those who have read widely in this field will find new ideas to stimulate their minds and hearts. The beauty of studying esoteric metaphysical traditions is finding the relatively few expositions that resonate with one, that ring true somehow. On the mountain, there is only one peak. But the paths leading to it are many!

The Ringing Cedars Series is not exactly a literary experience. The writing is rather poor, particularly in the early volumes, yet there's something extremely compelling about it. Author Vladimir Megre begins with the story of his fateful meeting with Anastasia, and we learn her secrets of gardening, child-rearing and healing. In later books, Anastasia covers topics such as breast-feeding, the meaning of ancient megaliths, the causes of war, the proper way to conceive a child, the origins of religion, and the creative potential of humanity. Her ideas on sexuality also differ greatly from conventional thinking.

One of the best aspects of Anastasia's philosophy of life is that it forces one to re-examine one's own philosophy. All too often we realize that our supposedly original opinions were actually handed down from parents, peers, teachers, or culture. One result of this phenomenon is the so-called "generation gap"–when cultural and philosophical norms change direction and cause head-on collisions between a society's youth and its older members.

As an example, one need only look as far as our public school system. The toe-the-line mentality of my parents' day, and of my own day to a certain extent, was no picnic; surely those hours wasted in regurgitating useless information could have been better spent. Today, the old-school, discipline-oriented approach has been completely replaced by the equally perverse emphasis on bolstering a child's self-esteem. In itself, there's nothing to criticize in that laudable goal. The problems only show up when the method of achieving it hinges on pyrrhic praise and abstention from correcting misdeeds.

Meanwhile, teachers are still forced to teach "to the test'" rather than stimulating children's curiosity and desire to learn by using activities that promote independent thinking. Being that a society of independent thinkers is the last thing any government wants, this is completely understandable.

The topic of Education is covered in Book 3 of the Ringing Cedars Series, in which Vladimir visits a remarkable Russian school where pupils construct their own buildings, study dance, music and martial arts, and cover the rest of the ten-year Russian school curriculum in two years. Students who are more advanced in a subject teach it to others, regardless of whether they are older or younger. The system was documented in a fascinating 2007 video called *The School: Humanity's New Future*. In one scene, an older student makes the following remarks:

*"I had a beautiful experience regarding a
biology class. We were studying cell
division. A boy named Dima was seated
next to me, around 12 years old. I was
interested in the subject. I had already
delved into it at university but at the time I
had not understood this topic fully. I could*

*not understand how the process of cell
division is done–how chromosomes
function, how individual cytoplasms are
divided, these kinds of details. He was
looking for a way to explain it to me. . . he
tried as best he could to answer my
questions. I could see the fire in his eyes,
how he'd collected knowledge and how he
wanted me to understand. After that class,
I realized that I understood it. In that
instant, I understood how the division of
cells is done. This boy had imparted to me
what I had not got from high school or
university textbooks or from a university
professor."* – student at The School

The Anastasia books seem to be flying under the radar of U.S. readers, but do not be surprised if, in coming years, many people are not only reading and discussing the books, but also putting some of Anastasia's suggestions into practice. While the thought of hiring a member of the *Ursidae* family to babysit may not sit well with most people (even though good help is so hard to find) there are many other ideas that may well provoke a *duh!* moment. In the end, the appeal of this series is in its package of common sense, folk wisdom, and promotion of mutual respect and love amongst all living things. What's not to like?

The Ringing Cedars Series is not science fiction, although some parts may seem like it. Just when you think the stories couldn't get any more incredible, they do. Maybe it's all in the setup: readers are advised, immediately preceding the title page, to sequester themselves away from sounds of traffic, appliances, and other artificial noises. Natural sounds such as chirping birds or gently flowing streams as background, however, are okay. It also says that you will feel better after reading the books. And I did!

When one attempts to create an atmosphere free of artificial sounds, one realizes it's easier said than done. In the city, unless one has an anechoic chamber handy, one is S.O.L. And in the country, the quaintness of the crow's caw is oft interrupted by thy neighbor's chainsaw. Nevertheless, making the effort to create such a reading environment will reward one not only with better absorption of the material, but also with the health benefits acquired through experiencing a more tranquil space.

The above directive to the reader, which appears in every book in the Ringing Cedars Series, is much more than a simple guideline. It is an invitation to get involved with one of the series' major themes: taking action. This meme is never actually stated, merely implied by the stories of the various characters. In anyone's life, when there's dissatisfaction or when one wants something, action is required. Many brilliant ideas have burned out because they were never acted upon. (If this has ever happened to you, raise your hand.)

The "action issue" should answer the question of why-oh-why did Anastasia, the beautiful and reclusive muse of the series, pick that lout Vladimir to be the author of the books—and more incredibly—the father of her children? After all, Vladimir behaves rather despicably on many occasions. But he is willing to display this aspect of himself as he tells the story, unlike many autobiographical authors. He's also a bit stubborn and rather dense, albeit enthusiastic.

As for his credentials, Vladimir is a businessman, captain of a trading ship. He has no writing experience. And to top it all off, he's already married! Thus the reader is continually confronted with the dichotomy of the central characters: the veritable goddess Anastasia, embodiment of perfection, and Vladimir the unenlightened boor whose redeeming features are not readily apparent. The verbal attacks on him in readers' letters (included in some of the books), and at speaking engagements, compel him to write more than a few paragraphs defending himself.

What Vladimir does have is the ability to act. His devotion to Anastasia and her message is his North Star, guiding him even as his obsession with writing the books destroys his business and leaves him destitute and homeless. Yet it's only through losing everything that he gains health, wealth and much more, and becomes happier and more successful than he ever thought possible.

Vladimir is the practical, grounding force that is so necessary to carrying out plans in the world of daily affairs. He asks the tough questions—the questions that critics and detractors will invariably ask as they try to foil the dreams and wreck the message of light and love that Anastasia wants everyone to receive. All of Vladimir's qualities turn out to be exactly those necessary to create the world that Anastasia says is Man's birthright–one domain at a time.

Kin's domains are a central theme of the series. Part of Anastasia's great plan is that everyone on Earth should have their own family domain, consisting of at least 1 hectare (about 2.5 acres) of land with a dwelling, trees, wild shrubs like berry bushes, and a garden to grow vegetables. If you lack a green thumb, never fear–Anastasia is full of information on planting and cultivation, as well as proper nutrition and other health-related issues. It is up to Vladimir to interest the politicians and petition the government to grant each Russian citizen their own hectare of land, free of charge. Meanwhile, the idea of the kin's domains has inspired thousands of real life Russian citizens to set up domains on their own, often in community settings of like-minded individuals and families.

A remarkable character in the series is Vladimir and Anastasia's son Volodya. Volodya is clearly a superior being from the reader's perspective, yet he shows the utmost respect and love for his father. Vladimir provides the needed role of advisor on the outside world, where the son must go in order to seek his future. He knows his destiny is not to remain in the *taiga* , but to venture into the world and help the people there. He asks his parents to create a little sister for him; the role of the sister is that she will take over Volodya's training of the forest animals, who are evolving through their relationship with humans. The sister, therefore, comes into the world with a clearly defined purpose for her existence, in contrast to most children born in the modern world.

In days of yore, a child's purpose was clear: to care for the parents in their old age, to contribute to the family by working, to maintain or even expand the family estate. Those of the upper classes married and produced offspring in order to perpetuate their line and their holdings. In lower economic classes, children helped with chores, got jobs, and cared for aging relatives. It was also not unheard-of for children to be sold as slaves, a practice which has never totally disappeared.

In the United States, poor parents can benefit financially from their children when the State dispenses stipends for their care. A rather offensive (but funny) popular joke (please note this is not from the book!) illustrates the latter: A woman with fifteen sons has named each of them "John." When she calls out "John!" they all come running. "What if you want to call them individually?" someone asks. "Oh," she replies, "then I just call them by their last names."

Children figure prominently in the Ringing Cedars Series. Their upbringing, education, innate abilities, even the proper conditions for their conception are topics appearing throughout all nine books. Education, in particular, is covered extensively; not only as it relates to the upbringing of children, but also to the ongoing learning that all individuals must pursue in order to stay vibrant and interested in life.

Anastasia says, "Every Man (this word, capitalized, refers to any human being) is so constructed that he has access to the whole Universe–both visible and invisible. Every Man may communicate with anything or anyone he wishes." Anastasia does not favor the sort of learning that is prevalent in most schools. She emphasizes that when information is received by someone, it must be more than just an intellectual idea. Rather, it must evoke feeling or emotion, or sensations of warmth, of fragrance, of sound. "When one experiences a vivid feeling, a large amount of information passes through Man in a flash . . . a correct complex of feelings sequenced in the right order can multiply a Man's existing store of knowledge by a thousandfold."

Some of the science fiction-like scenes in the books actually echo current research in reputable scientific circles. One such scene has a little girl disarming nuclear missiles by using her mind and her energy. Another scene shows Volodya holding a radioactive rock in his hand. He has taken it from the bottom of a lake, but is unable to let go of it because it will explode upon contact with the air. His mother talks him through a process of gradually releasing the rock's nuclear energy until it dissipates completely and the rock is rendered harmless. Volodya then concocts a plan for eliminating all the world's nuclear waste. He and that little girl are not alone in their quest–today's scientists are developing methods of transforming radioactive matter into inert substances.

Another important theme of the series is that of *Images*. According to Anastasia, certain images were created by an unseen ruling class (this part will appeal to conspiracy theorists) for the manipulation of people over the ages. As an example, she cites the Christian crucifix. This image is universally recognized all over the world yet few stop to examine its true origin. As a Symbol, the crucifix represents the suffering of Christ and his martyrdom for the sake of Humanity. As an Image, it has held vast numbers of people in dominion for 2000 years.

The image of the crucifix was not chosen by Jesus Christ, it was chosen by others. Who, where, why, and how? The day Christ was crucified was, one assumes, the worst day of his life. Why would someone who had spent his entire life serving his Creator, teaching mankind, healing the sick, spreading a gospel of Love and obedience to higher truths, want to be remembered by the day he was nailed to a cross and left on a hilltop to die along with common criminals? Doesn't make sense. Anastasia suggests that by selecting the image of the crucifix to be planted in the minds of untold millions of people for hundreds of years, those people could be manipulated and controlled by those who understood the laws of metaphysical imaging.

Neither does Anastasia shy away from other controversial topics, such as terrorism. She has her own take on 9-11, including a story not heretofore covered in any book, film or article on the subject, to my knowledge.

Shakespeare it ain't—but film producers should take note that *Star Trek* meets *The Secret* in The Ringing Cedars Series, which boldly goes where other books do not. Read on, Macduff.

♪

ARE YOU INSANE

IN 1973 A PSYCHIATRIST named David Rosenhan published the results of his highly controversial experiment of sending sane people into psychiatric hospitals with fake symptoms. The article was titled "On Being Sane in Insane Places," and it described how Rosenhan and several collaborators got themselves admitted into twelve such hospitals in five states, in various regions of the U.S., by saying they heard voices in their heads. Once they were admitted, they acted normally and told staff they no longer heard the voices, felt fine, and asked to be released. No dice. Almost all the collaborators had been diagnosed as schizophrenic, based on their made-up claim of auditory hallucinations.

Once admitted, the pretend-patients immediately began taking notes on their experiences in the hospital, secretly, lest their true identities became apparent. Then, emboldened by the fact that no one seemed to care, they began taking notes publicly. Yet the only ones who could tell that these were fake patients were the actual patients, who would approach them with comments like "You're not crazy. What are you doing here? Are you a journalist?"

Even more amusing (one must laugh to keep from crying) was the staff's re-framing of normal activities to correspond with the patients' diagnoses, as in this excerpt from Rosenhan's paper: "The facts of the case were unintentionally distorted by the staff to achieve consistency with a popular theory of the dynamics of a schizophrenic reaction . . . 'Patient engaged in writing behavior' was the daily nursing comment on one of the pseudo-patients who was never questioned about his writing. Given that the patient is in the hospital, he must be psychologically disturbed. And given that he is disturbed, continuous writing must be a behavioral manifestation of that disturbance, perhaps a subset of the compulsive behaviors that are sometimes correlated with schizophrenia." Rosenhan's summary: "It is clear that we cannot distinguish the sane from the insane in psychiatric hospitals."

On January 10, 2010, the New York Times Sunday Magazine published an article by Ethan Watters titled "The

Americanization of Mental Illness." The author discusses the control held by the American Psychiatric Association (APA) by virtue of its Diagnostic and Statistical Manual (DSM-IV), the world standard for categorizing and treating mental illness. The author points out that until a disorder like anorexia, for example, was promoted in this manual, it was virtually unheard of in countries other than the U.S. The manual lists hundreds more behaviors that are now classified as diseases.

Coinciding with the increasing power wielded by this faction of the APA is a counter-movement sometimes referred to as Anti-Psychiatry. One of the founders of this movement is Dr. Thomas Szasz, Professor Emeritus of Psychiatry at SUNY Syracuse and Lifetime Fellow of the APA. He says "no behavior or misbehavior is a disease, or can be a disease. That's not what diseases are."

Diseases have to be verified by blood tests, CAT scans, x-rays and other procedures that detect physical and chemical abnormalities. Mental illnesses, by contrast, are voted into existence by a committee. They are then listed in the DSM and assigned codes that are used to access the medical administrative system, the pharmaceutical system, and the insurance system.

Dr. Szasz comments, "If you talk to God, you are praying; If God talks to you, you have schizophrenia." Apparently Moses and Jesus, were they alive today, would be in serious trouble. Of course there are abnormalities of the brain that may benefit from treatment with pharmaceuticals or other methods. But how does one justify the draconian attempt to regulate the slightest "antisocial" behavior with forced drugging, electroshock treatments, or institutionalization–cures promoted by the medical establishment in the past, and currently.

Looking at history, we can see that declarations of mental illness have been used as an excuse to lock up many people who dared to disagree with the way things were being done. Runaway slaves in the 1850s; the suffragists in 1917; Russian political dissidents in mid-20th century, and Chinese dissidents today are just a few examples. Once someone is labeled defective it's easy to remove that person from his or her family–not to mention property and bank accounts–and the press.

See if the symptoms for Attention Deficit Hyperactivity Disorder (ADHD), the disorder du jour in American schools, don't describe just about every kid you've ever known:

• *the individual has difficulty sustaining attention*
• *is easily distracted*
• *often does not seem to listen*
• *often shifts from one uncompleted activity to another*
• *often loses things necessary for tasks*
• *often interrupts or intrudes on others*
• *has difficulty awaiting turn in groups*
• *often blurts out answers to questions*
• *often engages in physically dangerous activities without considering the consequences*
• *often talks excessively*
• *has difficulty playing quietly*
• *has difficulty remaining seated*
• *often fidgets or squirms in seat*
• *has difficulty following instructions.*
(Where eight or more of these apply, ADHD is likely to be present.)

Here's a thought: instead of putting kids on Ritalin, why don't we get them karate lessons and drum sets?

Let's consider some other folks who don't necessarily conform to the usual social behaviors–artists, writers and musicians. Dmitri Shostakovich, Bud Powell, Salman Rushdie, Aleksandr Zhdanov, Nawal El Saadawi and Camille Paglia are a few who come to mind. If the voices of original thinkers and creators like these were to be quashed, I would fear for humanity's future.

Trauma, fear, crises of faith, and the struggle to reconcile the primitiveness of our feelings with appropriate social behavior are all processes that are necessary in becoming a mature individual. Attempts by governments (or other agencies of control) to erase these processes from society through micromanaging the behavior of their citizens will result in bland societies indeed–the sort we have seen portrayed in countless films and novels depicting possible scenarios of the future.

Many third world countries have ceremonies, rituals and practices that address the need of a person's spirit to grow and to learn. Meditation, tribal music, dancing, and the ingesting of hallucinogenic plants are just a few of these. As Jesus says in the Gospel of Thomas [from the *Nag Hammadi Library*] "If you bring forth what is within you, what you bring forth will save you. If you do not bring forth what is within you, what you do not bring forth will destroy you."

Allowing people to experience what is within themselves in a protective, nurturing and controlled setting, such as a tribal circle or other sacred ceremony, seems like a better idea than feeding us drugs and putting us in state facilities when we don't march to the tune being blasted over the loudspeakers.

♪

SIZE MATTERS

AS HISTORICAL ERAS COME and go, so do their customs. Everything from conceptions of morality to clothing design is adopted, rejected and bellicosely debated whenever a new Zeitgeist emerges. Regarding clothing design, feminist pundits have been railing for years on the fashion industry's trend toward slimming its models down to a precious few pounds. They argue that women were never meant to be that thin, as evidenced by the more portly portrayals of the feminine figure in painting and sculpture through the ages.

In the United States, a country that loves to seesaw between yin and yang whenever possible, the issue has entered the mainstream agenda all the way up to the Federal level with Michelle Obama's "war on childhood obesity." Conversely, there is a faction that will defend to the death its right to be fat. This faction even has its own pin-up girls in the persons of Gabourey Sidibe and Mo'Nique, stars of the Oscar-winning film *Precious*.

If the plethora of food-related websites, TV programs, products and advertisements is any indication, it would seem that humans are pretty obsessed with the topic. A recent newspaper headline concerned a study by two graduate students on the increase in portions depicted in chronological renderings of the Last Supper. Apparently artistic license was used to beef up the servings, putting more emphasis on the aesthetics of the event rather than its original meaning–but that's a whole other can o' worms.

Never mind that the traditional daily meal of sages throughout antiquity consisted of fairly simple foods like bread or a bowl of rice. (For those engaged in warfare, maybe an occasional mastodon rib.) Those grad students may well be correct in their hypothesis that a Babette's Feast-sized Last Supper is probably stretching things in terms of historical accuracy.

Bringing the theme of size back to this author's home turf, another victim of history's size wars has been our poor little chromatic scale–the one that supplies the notes we use in Western European-derived music. (Unless you're a fan of music from Asia,

Africa or the Middle East, Western European music is pretty much all you'll ever hear.)

I'm constantly amazed by how big a half step–the smallest interval in Western music–really is. There's so much room between C and C#! Let me explain: the notes of the chromatic scale, in Western music, are regulated by a tuning system called *equal temperament*, adopted as the standard tuning only around two hundred years ago. Before equal temperament became the standard, there were many other tuning systems vying for supremacy. The basic characteristic of equal temperament is that all twelve tones are the same distance apart.

Other tuning systems, by contrast, usually rely on the intervals found in the all-natural, 100% organic *overtone series* (also referred to as the *harmonic series*). The overtone series is the aural equivalent of the rainbow. Just as the rainbow you see in the sky looks the same as the one seen by the very first human on earth, the overtone series is also the same as it's always been. It is natural, and immutable. In this aural rainbow, the intervals generated are NOT evenly spaced, so you can't change the key of the song without messing everything up. Even though other tunings sound weird to us–because we're not used to them–it's actually the man-made equal temperament scale that's out of tune!

The modern piano depends upon equal temperament for its tuning, and no one will deny that there has been–and continues to be–a wealth of great music created using equal temperament. But in olden days, each key had its own "color" and feeling. That's why composers included the key when they named their pieces: e.g. *Symphony No. 7 in A Major, Sonata in E Minor, Concerto in F.*

To make things even more complicated, wind instruments–which depend upon the overtone series for their very structure and operation–had to be pitched in different keys. You still see concert band and orchestral parts labeled *Clarinet in Bb* or *Horn in F.* Before the 19th Century not all instruments could play together, and it wasn't possible to change the key of the piece because that would render it screechingly unplayable. Equal temperament changed all that. While it's not a perfect system, it does make things a lot easier. For one thing we can all play music together now, and we can change the key of the song and it will still work. With standardization of pitch we've gained a great deal of flexibility . . . but what have we given up in exchange?

I believe one of the reasons for our fascination with Nature is that in a field of daisies, for example, not only the flowers themselves but also the centers, petals and stems are of different sizes. (The invisible roots are even more striking in their individuality.) Were the daisies all exactly the same, it would be a dead giveaway that we'd be looking at a fake field! Similarly, the natural overtone series gives us differently sized intervals, not just half steps and whole steps that are all the same.

As the art of music evolved, a startling paradox arose that threatened to undermine the entire arrangement. When harpsichords or organs were tuned so that they could consistently produce sounds corresponding to one of the venerable formulas, they were rendered incapable of playing the others. No instrument with fixed, unbending notes such as a piano can accommodate them all. Thus, certain combinations of tones that should have sounded sweet and placid could, on an early keyboard instrument, become sour and ragged. In search of a solution, musicians began to temper, or alter, their instrument's tunings away from the ancient ideals. The final solution-today's equal temperament-abandoned most of the revered musical proportions altogether. –from the book *Temperament* by Stuart Isacoff

When groups of instruments or voices (particularly in small ensembles) are not held to the rigid structure of the piano's equal temperament, they tend to gravitate more toward the natural tuning of the overtone series. Unlike the piano, voices and wind and stringed instruments can make tuning adjustments quite easily.

Keep in mind that while the equal tempered tuning system and its corresponding instruments are used worldwide, there are many other tuning systems and instruments in existence–like the ones found in countries such as China, Japan, Indonesia, Persia (Iran), India, and the African continent. That's why the indigenous music of those countries sounds so different to us. Then there are Western *microtonal composers* like Harry Partch and LaMonte Young who also make use of the many other notes that can be squeezed into an octave. In the words of composer and critic Kyle Gann, "May a hundred thousand scales flourish."

Perhaps because jazz music's roots stem from both Europe and Africa, it utilizes pitch inflections on purpose. Music *notation*, however, is a strictly European system and therefore does not include them. So we had to invent them! When you see the written music for a jazz piece, you might notice certain markings preceding and following the actual notes. The markings indicate that the pitch of the note should be altered by the player to create effects like the *bend*, *scoop*, or *fall-off*, to name a few. In written music, those effects can't be notated exactly because the pitches they create fall between the notes that are available to us in standard notation. But just because we can't see them doesn't mean they don't exist!

In music, as in life, one size does not fit all. Equal temperament might be the musical equivalent of the Euro–reducing tonal currency to a common denominator while drawing a line of demarcation in the sands of time. Dare you to step over it.

♪

SOUNDING OFF

WHAT'S THAT BEEPING? Is it time to take my vitamins, or is a truck backing up into my living room? Are my hard boiled eggs done? Oh, never mind–it's just on the TV.

We are surrounded by sound. How surrounded are we? We are so surrounded that we ignore most of those sounds, whereas sound's opposite–silence–commands our instant attention.

Silence is respect, as in *a moment of silence*. It's frightening: *an eerie silence descended upon the valley*. It's a symbol of power: *the group's performance silenced the critics*. It's a metaphor for death: *he must be silenced*. How interesting that a word representing stillness, the void, and emptiness should be so full of meaning. Yet the idea of silence that most readily comes to mind, in today's world, would probably refer not to the absence of all noises, just man-made ones.

Temporarily fleeing human and mechanical noise has always been a good idea, and now we're hearing much more sound and fury over the subject. In the New York Times Book Review of May 20, 2010, Ted Conover discussed three books touting the merits of this type of silence. He speculates that three writers coming out with books on silence, all within the space of a month, may indicate a "sonic tipping point." He notes that as a result of their research, each author–himself included–realized that silence is not, as one might think, nothing. Indeed, Grammy Award-winning musician Evelyn Glennie–who happens to be deaf–comments in the film *Touch the Sound* that "silence is probably one of the loudest sounds and heaviest sounds that you are ever likely to experience." Those fortunate enough to have reveled in rare moments of true silence would doubtless agree.

In a famous anecdote, composer John Cage related his discovery that even in a completely soundproofed *anechoic chamber* one still hears two sounds: the low drone of one's own circulatory system, and the higher pitched hum of one's nervous system. That jibes with quantum physics: the observer cannot be separated from the thing observed. On our quest for quiet we will have to take ourselves with us.

Thomas Edison is known to have been severely hearing-impaired. He could hear only the loudest noises. Being that he was the creator of significant communication inventions such as the phonograph (which, in its original incarnation, was both a recording and playback device), one would think he would have invented a hearing aid. Edison, however, was rather fond of not being distracted by "the babble of ordinary conversation." Not that a hearing person would wish to be deaf, but when the whole world starts sounding like a public school lunchroom at 11:45 a.m. it might be time to sign up for that meditation retreat.

Daily life drowns out truth with its busy, chit-chatty banality. As the theme song to the 1960s TV show *Mister Ed* (featuring a talking horse) told us, *People yakity-yak a streak and waste your time of day; but Mister Ed will never speak unless he has something to say!*

The planet we live on was already filled with its own smells, sights and sounds before the man-made ones came along. And just when it seems as if the world is so full we can't cram in another thing, along comes more. None of it ever goes away; it just keeps piling up.

As we seek balance, new products purportedly give us the nothingness we crave, in the form of less work and more leisure time. Of course, all that new nothingness needs accessories. For when we accessorize we bolster the illusion of having control over our lives.

A recent player on the accessory scene is the electric car. One of the most salient, and desirable, features of the electric car is the fact that it makes very little noise. Unforeseen Problem (don't you just love those): one of the ways that pedestrians, bicyclists and blind people avoid getting hit by cars is by hearing them coming. The electric car industry is addressing this problem by adding fake car noise to the vehicles (this is on the same order as the new electric fireplaces that come with a recording of crackling logs, contributing that final touch of realism the customer craves).

Someday in the near future you will go to the car wash and be able to buy not only a spray bottle of New Car Smell, but also an mp3 of Four Cylinder Strut. Simply insert it into the stereo, and it comes out the radiator grill! (Comparisons to the decline of the ancient Roman Empire notwithstanding, our simulacra and simulations beat their *lares* and *penates* any day of the week.)

Your new electric car will naturally be equipped with an alarm—despite the alarming preponderance of them in the last decade or two. Like the Boy Who Cried Wolf, the alarms have very poor judgement when left to their own devices. By the time we need the alarm it's either ignored or disabled, as happened in the BP/Transocean explosion in the Gulf of Mexico—only one of many disabled-alarm tragedies in recent years.

In our imperfect world, perhaps the best we can do is create space in our lives to listen to whatever faint voice of Truth may be broadcasting at the moment. As I listen now, I rotate my dial to the Memory Channel, and tune in to a junior high school band rehearsal. Mr. Burbank, our band director, is speaking. I can just barely make it out . . . he's saying . . . *don't play during the rests.*

♪

SPINNING WHEEL

IN THE PAST, the event known as Pearl Harbor was given short shrift in Japan's history textbooks. Likewise gone missing was Unit 731, the infamous Japanese biological and chemical warfare unit that conducted lethal experiments on humans during the war years of 1937-1945. No pages were spared, however, in depicting Japan as the victim in World War II after the bombing of Hiroshima and Nagasaki.

Tsk tsk, those naughty Japanese history book writers, withholding the truth from their nation's innocent schoolchildren. That would never happen in the United States! Why, when we were kids, we learned all about how the white people gave smallpox-infected blankets to the Native Americans, and how we interned Japanese-Americans in prison camps during World War II, and the Tuskegee Experiment, and the McCarthy Era . . . didn't we? On second thought, maybe we got that stuff from the bus driver. But in the classroom, we definitely learned about the really important historical figures like Napoleon, who said *What is history but a fable agreed upon.*

Some may argue it's entirely appropriate for a country's history textbooks to portray that country in a favorable light, emphasizing the laudable actions of its people. As Washington Irving remarked, *To illustrate the glory of his nation is one of the noblest offices of the historian.* On the other hand, Voltaire was of the opinion *The great horrors of the past are very useful. One cannot remind oneself too often of crimes and disasters.* But our Founding Father Benjamin Franklin said, *Indeed the general tendency of reading good history must be, to fix in the minds of youth deep impressions of the beauty and usefulness of virtue of all kinds.* Sheesh, now I'm really confused.

History's spotlight swings like a drunk on a lamppost, illuminating the Most Unlikely to Succeed just as often as the Destined For Greatness. Indeed, the writer Spalding Gray thought celebrities and ordinary people equally interesting, and would stage events during which he interviewed the latter to demonstrate it. The revered medievalist Eileen Power also believed that students would benefit from the study of "the lives of ordinary people" in order to effectively communicate the feeling of past times. "It is an illusion to think we can ever know what really happened; but it is a necessary and beneficial illusion," said Power.

With the proliferation of print and the advent of broadcast media, soon history was being rewritten even as it was being made. So frequent were the rewrites that the practice gained a one-syllable nickname: Spin.

The story of Helen Keller was an early example of spin. Generations of schoolchildren were regaled with tales of Keller (1880-1968), the blind and deaf girl who (with the aid of her teacher and companion Annie Sullivan) became a spokesperson and champion for people with disabilities. While Keller's achievements were ready-made for the press, there was one teensy little banana peel in the path: She was–gasp–a Socialist! To make matters worse, she was in favor of contraception; she wrote about the socially taboo subject of the association between blindness and venereal disease; she donated to the NAACP (Keller was a white woman from a wealthy Alabama family); she was a founding member of the American Civil Liberties Union; she trafficked with the controversial mystic Emanuel Swedenborg; and she opposed U.S. involvement in World War I, touring the country in support of American neutrality. Yet the pop version of Helen Keller we were taught in school focused exclusively on her triumph over her handicaps, with no mention made of the radical political beliefs which were the driving force in her life.

According to Bernard Grun's *The Timetables of History*, the first exactly dated year is -4241. Now we're in the 21st century, carrying all that history on our shoulders like Atlas. For a change of pace, we set it down and roll it uphill, like Sisyphus.

It takes a lot of fortitude to slice into history's leathery traveling trunk and rearrange things, but some people are doing it. One of them is the legendary chess champion Garry Kasparov. If you're looking for a smart guy, look no further. Among Kasparov's many achievements was a rather famous 1996 event: in a real John Henry moment, he defeated the IBM supercomputer Deep Blue in a much-publicized chess match (only to lose the rematch a year later, after Deep Blue had been souped-up). In his spare time,

Kasparov's prodigious, calculating mind was attracted to the work of Anatoly Fomenko, the Russian revisionist who states that the ancient history we've all been taught is off by over 1000 years. Other scholars have refuted his theories. Nevertheless, one is reminded of the old adage *even a stopped clock is right twice a day.*

Author Barbara Tuchman notes, "A greater hazard built into the very nature of recorded history, is the overload of the negative: the disproportionate survival of the dark side, evil, misery, contention, and harm . . . the normal does not make news." In that light, perhaps Oscar Wilde's assertion that *the one duty we have to history is to rewrite it* makes sense. It couldn't hurt to throw in a few nice, heartwarming stories to balance out all the horror. After all, we don't want to scare the kiddies.

Bad spin can happen to good people, and it frequently has to do with what's left out of the story. As Shakespeare reminds us via Marc Antony, *the evil that men do lives after them; the good is oft interred with their bones.*

When Jesus of Nazareth came on the scene a bit later, he inspired many scribes to document his life and teachings; thus began the struggle to gain control of early Christianity. In an attempt to ensure that certain dead men of Jesus' time would tell no tales, many "original" Biblical chapters were buried in upper Egypt, not to emerge until 1945 when they were accidentally discovered by locals digging around the limestone caves. These chapters were then translated and are known today as the *Nag Hammadi Library*. It seems rather fitting that these beautiful, spiritual writings are able, through only the power of words and ideas, to correct the sins of omission that occurred so many centuries ago.

Going back even further, our historical narrative's emphasis on "hunter" in the hunter-gatherer Paleolithic society colored everything that came after. The scholar and author Riane Eisler has taken on the task of reviewing written history from a feminine perspective, uncovering some viable alternative versions in the process. Her 1987 book *The Chalice & The Blade* opens with an acknowledgement of her mentor Alexander Marshack, a historian who investigated the Paleolithic cave drawings in France. He was the first person to write that the "weapons" depicted on the cave walls could just as easily be trees, branches and plants instead of spears, barbs and harpoons.

If we were willing to go back and reassess our ideas of history (You mean cavemen worshipped plants and goddesses? Really?) how much richer our human lineage could become. Untold insights could occur to us if we were willing to pry open the locked, rusty doors that hide treasures of knowledge and possibility from today's collective consciousness.

Revisionist vistas down memory lane may be the only weapon we have against Spin. Yet in our current surrealistic, Baudrillardian society, the revisions themselves also qualify as spin, reflecting as they do the agendas of their authors.

If our only choice is to fight spin with spin, then Truth–and Reality–will be sucked into the vortex as a consequence. What to do? We certainly don't want Truth and Reality to go down the drain. Hmmm . . . when in doubt–outsource! We could consult the Shakers, who told us *by turning, turning, we'll come 'round right*. Johnny Mercer's "Girlfriend of the Whirling Dervish," however, might give us some different advice.

♪

TAKE THIS TOWN & SHOVE IT

IN THE SOLAR SYSTEM of nations, Denmark is Pluto– it's tiny, and you only hear from them once every 248 years. The nation did have fifteen minutes of fame, though, back in the 60s when the legendary Jazzhus Montmartre was swinging its way into jazz lovers' hearts. (The club closed in 1965, but reopened in 2010 under the management of Rune Bech and pianist Niels Lan Doky.)

Over fifty years ago, quintessential American jazz musicians Stan Getz, Ben Webster, Kenny Drew and many others moved to London, Amsterdam, Paris, Copenhagen, where they were welcomed as important artists. They had their health needs met (often free of charge) and the whole neighborhood said hello when they walked down the street. It was a marked contrast to life in their own country, where after working for decades perfecting their music, they had achieved artistic success and little else. Goodbye U.S.A., hello Europe.

I first became aware of the great tenor saxophonist Dexter Gordon in the late 70s, shortly after he had returned to New York after having lived in Copenhagen for fourteen years. While living abroad, Dexter (he was affectionately known by his first name whether you knew him or not) played dates in his home country but spent most of his time in Europe. In a DownBeat Magazine interview he credited his adopted city of Copenhagen with his development as an artist: "[Living here] has been very good because my whole lifestyle is much calmer, much more relaxed. I can devote more time to music, and I think it is beginning to show. It's not an everyday scuffle, and I'm able to concentrate more on studying."

But meanwhile, the city of Copenhagen was far less of a haven for some of its native sons and daughters. In 1971, a few years before Dexter returned to the United States, a group of Copenhagen residents took over an abandoned military compound in the middle of the city. With a vision of a "free" society that was self-sustainable and based on community values, they built homes, started businesses, and soon grew to be a commune of several hundred members. It still exists; it's called Freetown Christiania and is not ruled by the city, the country, or the European Union. It attracts a half million tourists annually. Now, as then, there are no cars, guns, or hard drugs allowed there. Also not allowed–and this may be the defining issue for Christianians–is the selling, buying, or trading of houses. When one wants to move, one simply packs up and leaves.

Transportation is by foot, bicycle, wagon, and horse. A use fee of a few hundred dollars per month is pooled from residents, and this is used to buy services like water and electricity from the Danish government. It is a walled-off, bucolic oasis smack dab in the middle of a hustling metropolis.

The community of Christiania has existed since 1971, but there are regular attempts by the Danish government to take control over the area. It's not any surprise that since Christianians have made this section of Copenhagen a major tourist destination, the powers-that-be now want it back. The usual reasons are cited, such as:

• Concern for the safety of Christiania residents (even though they're doing just fine, thank you very much).

• The original buildings are the property of the government (even though they were abandoned for years and became habitable only by virtue of their restoration by citizens, at their own expense).

It's like the old story Artists Fix Up The Place, Then Get Kicked Out. Perhaps the moral is to build these sorts of communities far away from cities, as was done at Findhorn in Scotland, or the Earthship Star community in New Mexico. (But as the continuing struggle of the *Zapatistas* in Chiapas, Mexico shows, the issue is never Location as much as it is Belief.)

Around the same time as the founding of Christiania, something interesting was happening in New Mexico. A renegade architect named Michael Reynolds decided there was no reason that you couldn't build a beautiful home completely out of natural and recycled materials, on cheap land, powered by wind and solar energy, using water from rain and snow melt, with an attached greenhouse for food production. The local authorities were, naturally, not too keen on this. After all, being off-the-grid means that the grid (and everyone who works for it) doesn't get paid.

Beleaguered by regional bureaucrats, Reynolds was denied building permits and even had his architect's license revoked. Most people would have given up, but Reynolds decided to change the system from the inside. He worked for many months preparing a State Senate bill that would allow "experimental housing." The first attempt at getting the bill passed was unsuccessful after a filibuster ate up the clock before his bill could be presented. At the next session, however, a sympathetic Representative was able to get enough support for the bill to get it passed.

The film *Garbage Warrior* tells the dramatic story of this courageous, iconoclastic and innovative man. The Earthship houses he invented have become models of low-cost, sustainable living. His team travels worldwide (often on a volunteer basis), teaching the locals how to build the much-needed shelters for themselves. These communities, separated not only by geography but also by other factors like religion or diet, have one thing in common: they have, either partially or fully, rejected the values espoused by their countries' governments. They also share a philosophy: do no harm to others while seeking life, liberty, and the pursuit of happiness. If my understanding of American History is correct, this is exactly what the Founding Fathers had in mind.

Perhaps there really is a silent majority that believes in helping themselves through helping others; having land with which to cultivate one's own food; having the right to drink clean water; the right to have an education, the right to live alongside those who share one's basic values.

The fact that hundreds of self-governing communities exist worldwide is not generally known. While I myself am not necessarily off to live in one next week, it does give me comfort to know they're there.

We have many laws designed to protect mankind from itself–with new ones being passed daily. Yet man continues to prey on his own kind, and laws don't help. Many large corporations seem to be nothing more than giant pyramid schemes, rife with inefficiency (except when skimming fortunes off the top) and having a goal of self-perpetuation rather than responsibility to the people they purport to serve. Modern society's increases in mental and physical illness, suicide, and drug use indicate there are more than a few individuals out there who feel lost in their lives.

Day-to-day difficulties tend to narrow one's focus to little more than oneself and one's family, yet there are places where one can change one's life and also be of service to others. Sometimes you can even get paid!

The Fellowship for Intentional Community lists over 900 communities in the United States alone. Some are in the boondocks, others are right in the middle of the city. There is scant press coverage of these remarkable organizations.

Environmental disasters, inflation, corporate crime, health challenges, foreclosures, public school crises and unemployment are all at a high point; a personal encounter with a single one of these issues could easily prompt someone to reassess his or her priorities.

It takes resilience, inventiveness and perspective to find a clear path to a fulfilling life. Walking this path, one meets others like oneself–those who, by virtue of courage or circumstance, were compelled to *just say no* to at least a few of the indignities and insanities of modern existence.

♪

THEY LIED TO US • PART I

IT WASN'T THAT LONG AGO but it seems like a whole 'nother era: the 1990s, which saw the rise of the *indie* musician. "Indie" was a nickname for "independent," as opposed to artists who had recording contracts. Up until then, most musicians had to make recordings through a label because of the high cost involved in making the product, vis a vis 1. Recording 2. Manufacturing 3. Distribution 4. Marketing. Keep these four stages in mind–we'll come back to them later.

Some interesting things started happening. Home recording equipment got cheaper and better. This created a need for affordable indie manufacturing which was filled by companies such as DiscMakers and Oasis. The CDs that were manufactured needed distribution, and along came CD Baby, and middleman distributors like Artist One Stop and North Country that brought these CDs to stores like Barnes and Noble, Virgin Megastore, and Tower Records (which now exists only in certain international locations). The mystery of the barcode was decoded and made available to us commoners for tracking of sales by Sound Scan. Internet connections improved, and streaming audio and digital downloads became easier.

iTunes was born in April of 2003. All the brick and mortar retailers jumped on the bandwagon with their own download offerings, joining the increasingly popular (and increasingly profitable) Amazon dot com in offering mp3 versions of both major label and indie CDs. If you can't beat 'em, join 'em, thought the record labels, as they proceeded to buy up space on the playing field. It was then that the average lot size on the playing field started to shrink.

When I attended one of the first Future of Music Conferences in Washington, D.C. in the early 2000s, the phrase "level playing field" was served up more times than a tennis ball at Wimbledon. All the panelists seemed convinced that because the recording process was no longer locked up by the "majors," the indies would be able to bypass them and take control of the dissemination and sales of their music, reaping the profits thereof. Their plan worked perfectly–except for the profit part.

Because pressing a CD became so affordable, pretty soon anyone with a pulse, a credit card, and two notes to put together could make a CD–and they did. Hence, the recordings created by real musicians were thrown into the same hopper as everyone else's. There went the neighborhood! As CDs became numerous and ubiquitous, the value of your CD followed–in inverse proportion.

Meanwhile, the music consumer (your potential customer) was flummoxed. So many choices, so little time. Hello, Stage 4. We mentioned the stages earlier: recording, manufacturing, distribution, and MARKETING. The marketing stage is the tipping point, at which the so-called level playing field starts to tilt wildly. Because as we all know, people (even us, the enlightened ones) tend to go with what they know–or at least with what they've heard of. What sells? The stuff at eye level in the store display, the newspaper, the magazines, the web. Everything else sinks to the bottom, where the collective weight of it all makes a nice anchor to buoy up the top.

But what about the Grammy Awards, you ask. Isn't that a peer review process for all the professional CDs? Don't the best CDs win awards so music consumers will know what to purchase? As a former voting member of the Recording Academy, which produces the Grammys, let me enlighten you: There are hundreds of CDs on the Grammy ballot, in dozens of categories. You are supposed to vote only in your area of expertise, but even so, there are many, many albums, artists, compositions, solos, arrangements, and other categories in your field to vote on. The tracks on the ballot are not located on a central website where they can be heard by Recording Academy members. So you can imagine what happens–you end up voting for your friends, your personal favorite artists (regardless of whether you've listened to the track on the ballot), and the tracks you happened to hear on the radio that you liked. There are many other deserving tracks on the ballot that you will never hear.

Even if there were a practical way to actually listen to each track on the ballot, you would have to devote countless unpaid hours to reviewing them all and making an honest evaluation. Probably you would still end up voting for yourself, your friends, and your personal favorite artists. Maybe a few others would earn a little checkmark on your ballot, which would then wing its way over to Deloitte & Touche to be counted. And maybe if all the voting members made an effort to listen to some of the tracks they were unfamiliar with, a few great musicians nobody has heard of would get a break.

In our un-perfect world, we rely on MARKETING as a substitute for actual listening. And marketing costs either money, or time, which is the same thing. Is it possible to circumvent the record companies and sell thousands of units on your own? Of course it is! The Internet abounds with such stories. So, those artists who have sold tons of CDs and digital downloads, how did they do it? By playing lots of live shows, and MARKETING. And, oh yeah–it helps to be good.

It was at the same Future of Music Conference mentioned earlier that I met the Australian film and TV composer Charlie Chan, who told me she was no longer even making physical CDs. She was ahead of the curve, but now more and more artists are going completely digital with their audio products. This particular conference is also where I first met CD Baby founder and superstar music business guru Derek Sivers. At one of the presentations, Derek was part of a panel. He was introduced by the moderator and the entire audience of mostly musicians gave him a screaming standing ovation. "Who the hell is THAT?" said the lawyer sitting next to me, clueless.

There you have it. Releasing a CD is only the beginning. The playing field is not level until your team puts in as many hours as the record company's team. If you cannot do that, then your product might be destined to be counterweight for the CD see-saw for as long as there are boxes of units cramping your closet. As one pundit sagely remarked–"even Coca-Cola still advertises."

♪

THEY LIED TO US • PART II

IN PART ONE OF "THEY LIED TO US" we got an overview of how the recording biz has changed (not necessarily for the better) over the past couple of decades. Now stop yer gripin'– because here we take a look at the new models of project financing and packaging for musicians. And while we're at it, let's examine the role of the Artist in Western society: what it is, and what it could be.

We can sing the blues about capitalism and free market economies all day long, but at the end of the day, the consumer gets what the consumer wants: free music. They're willing to pay for certain music, but they expect the freebies too. They feel entitled. Therefore, there will NEVER be an end to pirating, file sharing, bootlegging, or any other mode of disseminating free music.

The music field, by the way, is not the only one suffering from non-compensated loss of intellectual property. The trend is ubiquitous, and anyone who makes a living selling any sort of digital content is feeling it. The world of non-digital content, however, figured things out a long time ago. (Perhaps their products' location on the dense physical plane of the grocery shelf, as opposed to cyberspace, afforded a more grounded perspective.) It's a very simple formula. Step One: Get the customer into the store by marking down the paper towels (this is referred to as a *loss leader*). Step Two: Sell the customer some more stuff while he/ she is there, at the regular price. Or higher.

As discussed in Part I of this essay, musicians are desperately trying to step on whatever rocks may exist in the vast sea of entertainment marketing out there. Instead of complaining about this, real musicians can see it as an opportunity to separate themselves once again from the hoi polloi. In the old days we did this by obtaining a recording contract. Today, we use *bundled packaging*, which is a digital version of the loss leader concept. Because it's so easy to shoplift a download, cyber stores give them away as loss leaders. They use tiered pricing systems (Platinum level, Diamond level, Rhinestone level) and offer bundled packages to their customers, just as phone companies offer specially priced packages that include services like long distance calling and Internet access.

What is the difference between your music track—your musical baby—and a roll of paper towels? From a merchandising perspective, none. Who is to blame for this? Well, actually, WE MUSICIANS are. We allowed our music to be assigned a value by social economics, rather than insisting on a value that reflects our time, effort, creativity, skill, and expenses. It won't be easy to turn things around, but since creativity is our coin of the realm, we should use it to get ourselves out of this mess.

On the business model side, game-changer companies like ArtistShare, Indiegogo, Kickstarter and Patreon forge a relationship between artists and their fans, who will pay a premium for bundles of exclusive content from that artist. In exchange for contributions that fund an artist's current project, fans receive things like sheet music, rehearsal and performance videos, online lessons, and other behind-the-scenes glimpses of the creative process. They can "experience an artist's project from its conception to its fruition," in the words of ArtistShare Founder and President Brian Camelio. "At ArtistShare," he says, "we believe that the true value of an artist is their creative process . . . not the end result."

Indiegogo, Kickstarter and others do the same thing as ArtistShare but on a smaller scale. They are more like micro-financing sites, allowing fans to contribute with donations as small as a few dollars. The artists benefit from these business models not only financially, but also organizationally. They must plan out their projects using appropriate timelines, making regular progress updates in order to nurture the project and bring it to completion. Because the goal is clearly defined and the artist knows that her fans are actively following her, she can be even more focused and more creative. Patreon differs slightly in that it uses a subscription model, but the gist is the same.

Providing this sort of exclusive access will reward the artist whose work is above the fray. This is why I believe that crowdfunding sites like the ones mentioned above are the early adopters in what will surely become the standard model of artist funding as we proceed further into the 21st century.

Lest my comments suggest I'm advocating that music-making be restricted to professionals, let me clarify. Obviously, playing (and listening to) music is a beautiful thing that can be enjoyed and appreciated at all levels of ability, just like sports or any other activity. Western society's categorization of all music as entertainment, however, does a disservice to its people, and to music itself.

In tribal societies, musicians fill a vital role in ritual, ceremony and spiritual life, not just entertainment. In the West, however, we recognize Sacred Music only in the Judeo-Christian liturgical canon. Any music that purports to accompany meditation, healing or ritual is classified as either "World Music," or else "New Age music," a category that suffers greatly from lack of a Quality Control Department.

In the absence of well-defined roles for musicians in terms of what society expects from us, we have created the role of Artist. The Artist is our version of the Eastern guru, the shaman, the healer, the Native American medicine man, the South American *curandera.* The role of the Artist has always been to express the sublime, and to connect the listener/viewer/reader to forces beyond one's daily experience or access. Art is our backstage pass to other realms, other levels of reality. For how can we deepen ourselves as humans unless we reach for something beyond the quotidian Wake, Work, Play, Sleep cycle?

True Art provides a transformational experience. It is not an experience to be approached lightly. Yet when Art is seen only as entertainment, the Artist is forced to present his/her art in the same context as an entertainer. This de-values the experience of Art. This is not to say that Art can't be entertaining, or that entertainment can't be artistic. The co-mingling of the two, however, tends to remove the "sacred" element that is so necessary to the experience of inner transformation.

As a music professional for four decades and counting, I've observed a disturbing trend that seems to encapsulate the devaluation of music and musicians: the volume level. Music is being played louder and louder. I often enjoy the rehearsal for the gig more than the gig itself, because at the rehearsal we only use amplification to create a balance. On the gig, the entire shmagilla gets cranked up, and the dynamic levels that can range from *pppp* to *ffff* in an acoustic setting get reduced to low, norm and max. I don't know about you, but when I listen to music I want more fidelity than what I get from my air conditioner.

So do we need to have all our concerts outside in a pine grove while the audience sits around us in a circle, holding hands? That seems a bit reactionary. Rather, it simply behooves everyone who cares about music to start demanding quality, and the conditions for appreciating that quality.

My colleague Ken Hatfield has commented on this issue at length. He told me a story that illustrates his point beautifully: He was asked to play solo acoustic guitar as entertainment on a chartered flight. (This was an unusual request, and naturally the accompanying monetary figure reflected that.) Ken accepted the gig, but on one condition–he told the promoter that his performance must be presented as a concert, and not as background music! Ken's demand was accepted, he did the gig, people listened (engine noise notwithstanding) and everyone was happy. Most musicians would not have dared to make such a demand for fear of losing the gig. The favorable outcome was a result of Ken's personal commitment to presenting his music in the best possible light. This is a light that illuminates the experience for the listener, as well as the artist. Long may it wave.

♪

TRUMAN BURBANK'S STORY

IN 1998 A REMARKABLE movie came out. It was a film that simultaneously encapsulated modern life in America, and showed where we might be headed if we stay on our current trajectory. The film is called *The Truman Show*. In case you have not seen it, here's the spoiler: Truman (played brilliantly by Jim Carrey) lives on an island with a small town-suburban feel. His days follow a comfortable routine–buying the paper at the newsstand, going to work, drinking a beer at twilight with his best buddy. The back story: Truman will never leave the island, because the only way off is by boat and he's had a fear of water ever since his father drowned. He works for an insurance company and is married to a beautiful, airhead blonde. He always thought his life was very normal. Through an escalating series of coincidences, however, he is becoming aware there's something people are hiding from him.

The back story of the back story: Truman is the star of a reality television series called *The Truman Show*. It broadcasts 24/7. Everyone in the town is an actor and is being paid by the same corporation that adopted Truman when he was a baby and installed him on the set of this town, complete with actor parents, friends, and extras. Truman, of course, does not know that his every move is broadcast to a worldwide audience.

The 24/7 schedule gives ample time for product placements from the show's sponsors. If Truman's wife lingers a bit while holding up the box of laundry detergent, and mentions the strength of its cleaning power more often than necessary, well, Truman is used to it. Meanwhile, although *The Truman Show* television program has millions of devoted viewers who have been watching him his whole life, a *Free Truman!* counter movement has sprung up.

Have you ever wondered just why people make comments on the weather? Maybe that's because it's one of the big things in life that can't be controlled. Remarks like "beautiful day" or "it's a wet one today" contain traces of appreciation, of submissiveness, of acquiescence. But not on the set of *The Truman Show*, because

TERRY

the entire thing is under a giant dome with a canvas sky, and the weather is controlled by the show's Artistic Director.

Truman, finally sensing that things just don't add up, begins to plot an escape from the island. At first it's a vacation. But as the *Deus ex machina* (in the form of Cristof, the show's creator) continues to foil his every plan, Truman starts having a nervous breakdown and a reckless spree ensues. Overcoming his deathly fear of the sea, he launches a sailboat and sets a course for "anywhere but here." As Cristof (deftly played by Ed Harris) looks on from his control tower high above the set, he attempts to thwart Truman by sending foul weather to capsize the little boat. It seems that Cristof would prefer the show to come to a dramatic finish rather than see his star abandon it–even if Truman dies in the process.

Shouting "is that the best you can do?" to the unseen puppeteer, Truman regains control of the boat and weathers the storm, which has ended because of a staff mutiny in the control tower. In bright sunshine, our hero continues sailing toward the horizon. His journey comes to an unexpected end when he abruptly bumps into the canvas sky. He begins to move toward a door in the sky marked *EXIT* when he hears Cristof's voice entreating him to stay.

"Who are you?" Truman asks.

Cristof says gently, "I'm the creator of a TV show that gives joy and hope to millions of viewers all over the world."

"Then who am I," Truman asks.

"You are the star," Cristof replies. He tells Truman that the world he created for him is perfect–whereas the world outside is full of war and hate. Why would Truman want to leave? Realizing that his whole life has been immersed in a world of lies and deceit, in which his innocence was exploited for profit– Truman walks out the door. As the scene shifts to the various fans out in TV Land, cheers and cries of victory ring out as people hug one another and celebrate Truman's escape.

When the film first came out I had occasion to ask some teenagers what they thought of the idea of being constantly under observation. To my generation, the privacy issue was absolutely galling. Our electronic tether to the world has gained in strength as devices such as cellphones, RF tags, smart chips, OnStar emergency service, and GPS units are now standard equipment. Retinal scans and identity chips are already here as well. Privacy is regularly traded for "security," but somehow, we never feel any safer. But the young people in my informal survey were not fazed by this in the least. Wherefore this cavalier attitude? I realized that those born in the United States in 1982 would have spent their entire life being videotaped, photographed, and otherwise monitored—so the fact that the Truman character was under continuous observation elicited the response "so what."

The script of *The Truman Show* reads like a reality show written by philosopher Jean Baudrillard, who opined on the subject of copies becoming more "real" than the original. We invest emotion, energy and time into upholding the simulation, which then becomes the new reality. When reality shows come to us via backlit screens with moving images, the package is mesmerizing. Beats hell out of staring at stained glass!

The 1998 *Truman Show* film can be described as a story about the ultimate reality show. Television reality shows began in the early 1980s with programs like *That's Incredible* and *Real People*. Another show called *The Real World* aired in 1992. But the moniker *reality show* did not actually appear until the 2002 hit series *Survivor*. Ironically, it doesn't take long for reality show cast members to start acting, as they learn on the job how to play to the camera and the audience. It's probably inevitable that the complex bouquet of a real person be reduced to a "character" for presentation on the screen.

Adults using electronic drug to sedate their children – it's called "tele-vision" – induces states of stupidity and non-alertness, worst of all it brainwashes millions, some say billions of these moron zombies to believe anything they see or hear through the "tele-vision." This device claims to let you "see" things that are not in your living space and uses actors and visual stimulation to make you spend your money on crap

*you would never ever have thought to
buy otherwise. Makes you fat and
lazy, unmotivated and fearful of
everything "real" and promotes
moral relativism and sadomasochistic
behaviors.*
–comment on Wired Magazine
website: Posted by: Cosmicjaguar
08/2/10
4:29 p.m.

Additionally, the time structure of a typical television broadcast format exerts a certain power. Composer Derwyn Holder has a theory: the ubiquitous half-hour and hour-long TV time slots have programmed the nervous systems of regular viewers into expecting real life conflicts and dramas to come to a climax and a resolution according to this artificial schedule. When they don't, the participants may feel confused: "Why is this problem not ending now!" Like nightmares of being in a play but not having the script and not knowing one's lines, one may feel inadequate to the task at hand–living life.

But it's not all bad. Perhaps in our search to invent ever-smaller versions of ourselves that can be expressed with Internet avatars, or statements of 140 characters or less, as on Twitter–we have an unprecedented opportunity to discover our true essence. One can send a hologram of oneself out into cyberspace–a little morsel of our life that rings true, like a Zen koan. Avatars and tweets–diaphanous *doppelgängers*–are sent out to cyberspace-at-large as representatives of one's real self. There is also the advantage of being able to be many places at once, unlike that cumbersome physical body.

A tweet may speak of hunger–but it is not hungry. It speaks of pain–but it feels none. The bizarre twist of being human is that we keep returning to physical reality no matter how pain-filled it may be. One licks one's wounds like the animal one is. We eat, drink, breathe, touch; we interact with the universe around us. We ultimately seek the most basic, primal experiences because those are the actions that affirm our humanness. You can't eat a tweet.

Cristof couldn't understand why Truman would trade an "ideal life" for the pain, uncertainty and sordidness of regular, unregulated reality. But just like Neo in *The Matrix*, Truman wanted The Truth. That we have created films and TV shows which simulate truth is the very embodiment of the matrix: a consensus of reality that substitutes for the real thing so well that, like Plato's Cave, some people may no longer know what life is really like on the other side of the canvas sky, and indeed, may not be aware it exists at all. Others, meanwhile, are aware of feeling trapped inside a simulation. They seek Truman's exit door, or Neo's red pill.

My favorite line in *The Matrix* is when Cipher says, "I know this steak isn't real. But it tastes so good!" Meanwhile, back on the ship, Neo and the crew are eating slop. The "truth" may be highly overrated.

♪

WHAT'S YOUR SINE

WHEN I WAS ELEVEN years old I fell for one of my dad's practical jokes. It was a mellow Sunday morning and I was exploring his vinyl record collection to which I had recently been granted access. Between the Billy Taylor and J.J. Johnson 16 rpm Prestige sides I found an album with a plain white cover. On the label of the album was this handwritten note: *WARNING! NOT FOR CHILDREN.* Since I had to ask my dad's permission before I played any of his albums on the stereo, I went into the kitchen where he was reading the paper. "Dad, I found this album. Can I play it?" He glanced at the label and looked at me very seriously. "Wellllllllll," he said, "I guess you're old enough now. Go ahead."

Pleased that I had evidently graduated from child status, I gleefully skipped out to the living room to see what forbidden audio treasures awaited me. I carefully extracted the album from its plain white sleeve. I placed it on the turntable, lowering the stylus with anticipation. The familiar faint crackle of the vinyl grooves sounded, followed by an electronic tone. "160 hertz" a male voice said. Then a higher tone: "500 hertz" said the voice. More tones were sounded, along with the corresponding frequencies. I was confused. Back into the kitchen I went.

"Dad," I said, "I don't understand why this record is not for children."

I had never seen an adult go into paroxysms of laughter before, especially my father. He was cracking up. He was practically on the floor laughing. After he got his breath, which seemed to take forever, he gasped "it took fifteen years for that joke to pay off!" Apparently my dad, before he'd even married my mom, had thought it would be hysterical to someday fool his as-yet-unborn kid into listening to a hi-fi system test recording.

Those more innocent days seem far from today's Digital Age where altered states are just a click away. But back then, who knew there would be this craze known as *iDosing* in which young people don headphones and listen to binaural beat tracks designed to replicate brain waves produced by drugs like marijuana, cocaine and LSD?

Naturally, this fad is of some concern to parents and other gatekeepers. But since the idea that it's dangerous to lie motionless while listening to audio tracks through headphones is rather easily ridiculed, they emphasize (Reefer Madness-style) that such activities could lead to stronger, harder stuff.

In my view, rather than fret over the mind altering substance *du jour* our young people are sampling, why do we not ask what it is that our society is failing to provide its citizens? Whence the void that must apparently be filled by recreational intoxicants?

In contrast, a society with a metaphysical purpose at its heart, such as that of the Plains Indians of the 18th and 19th centuries for example, automatically offers a social role and a code of ethics to its members. All were expected to prepare themselves physically and mentally to receive at least one life-guiding vision that would provide protection and be a source of power, conferring a special wisdom not only for their personal benefit, but also for that of the tribe. Exceptional leaders, such as the Sioux Chief Crazy Horse, obtained his power through the solitary vision quests he performed several times each year. Inebriants like tobacco were not recreational items, but rather substances to be used for sacred purposes. The prevailing ethos with which children were raised was to be of service to one's people.

In his classic tome *The Mystic Warriors of the Plains*, Thomas Mails describes the daily mindfulness involved in belonging to such a society. How stark the contrast with our current era, in which our young people have been encouraged to focus on themselves. Like a TV spinoff series, this sort of self-referential preoccupation creates a loop whose integrity weakens with each revolution.

Youth is keenly aware of duplicity. When kids see adults who proclaim the evils of substance abuse even as they freely consume legal drugs like alcohol, tobacco, and prescription medications, they quite naturally click the mute button. When President Obama said "I inhaled frequently. That was the point. . ." he won the hearts of much of America's youth, for whom Change meant "straight talk and no more lies." But change is slow in coming, and many still seek the taste of *terra incognita* that forbidden drugs seem to provide.

That kids would turn to digital outlets for this should not be surprising. Also not surprising is the shock expressed by certain members of–for lack of a better term–the Establishment. Headlines such as *Can Kids Get High From the Internet?* display a disingenuous incredulity that is–let's just say it–revolting. Here's some real news for those people: you can get high from BREATHING. Indian yogis have been doing it for thousands of years. Not into breathing? No problem–go out for a jog and get yourself a runner's high. Endorphins are legal, and free! But be warned–they're addictive as hell! If running ever becomes a felony, we'll know why.

The debate over what is addictive (*physically and mentally dependent on something and unable to stop without incurring adverse affects; enthusiastically devoted to a thing or activity*) and what is not has far more to do with politics and power than it does with concern for the welfare of humanity. Food, sex, music, shopping, shoplifting . . . are any of these addictive per se? Nooooooo, but then again, anything is addictive if someone is addicted to it.

Regarding the iDosing phenomenon, it would seem that the most imminent danger faced by users isn't scrambled brain waves but hearing loss. Moreover, anyone truly seeking a transcendental audio experience need listen no further than, say, Stravinsky's "Rite of Spring" or the music of Hildegard von Bingen or Miles Davis. This truth was tacitly underscored by the Gates of Hades YouTube listener who commented "well that was 9:34 that i will never get back."

As professional musicians watch their livelihood erode with every free download, we have this to be thankful for: people are once again becoming aware of the power of sound. iDosing is merely one tangent; another is the renewed interest in the effects of sound waves, such as those generated by Chladni Plates or the 1960s and 70s Cymatics experiments of Hans Jenny. Vinyl is making a comeback, and so is vintage recording equipment. In the alternative health field, various modalities of Sound Healing are gaining popularity.

The use of music and sound to influence the workings of the human body has been an integral part of maintaining health in a variety of cultures for thousands of years. Did they know something we don't? There's only one way to find out.

♪

TIME IS EVERYTHING

I HAVE NOT WORN a wristwatch since December 14, 2009. That was the night my whole concept of Time was forever altered. I'll start by telling you what happened during the week prior to the date mentioned: I had traveled to a remote region of Peru to the hacienda of Shaman Diego and his wife Milagros. An international group of thirteen people had assembled there to take part in a series of sacred *ayahuasca* ceremonies. The ceremonies began at 8 p.m. and usually concluded around 2 a.m. or so. Like the old joke "I spent a week in Cleveland one night," I would look at my watch and it would be midnight; then an hour later I would look at my watch again and it would be 12:05. Hence my subsequent, and lasting, disillusionment with my formerly trusty Timex. Now I do what the kids do–get the time from my cellphone.

Newton (you know, the guy who invented the Fig Cookie) said that Time is absolute. Parmenides and Zeno said Time is unreal. Immanuel Kant said Time is neither an event or a thing and it can't be measured. Who, and what, should we believe?

In the Judeo-Christian and Age of Enlightenment traditions prevalent in the Western Hemisphere, time is considered to be a linear phenomenon. It marches on, and never does an about face. This concept is diametrically opposed to the view of the rest of the world which says time is cyclical. Civilizations for whom the latter was true include the Mayan, Incan, Aztec, Hopi, Ancient Greek, Hindu and Buddhist, among many others.

Physicists of the last hundred years have tended more and more toward the view that not only is time cyclical, but it is also simultaneous in the sense that it can run forward or backward–exceptions like the 2nd Law of Thermodynamics notwithstanding. We have Einstein to blame for this state of affairs. He destroyed the traditional idea of Time when he wrote about its undeniable relationship with Space. In a nutshell, it turns out that Space and Time had been sleeping together ever since the Big Bang. We were the last to know.

Pieces of time longer than one day are measured by calendars, while those of one day or less are measured with hours, minutes and seconds. A second can seem like a long time (especially at the Olympics, or when you're soloing on some chord changes you don't really know). In fact, the second had so much space, developers moved in and sectioned it off even further. These days, common parlance for a "split second" is the *nanosecond*–but there are other, even smaller, increments: try the *picosecond*, the *femtosecond*, or the *attosecond* on for size.

Once upon a time, the unit of time known as the "second" was based on a mathematical division of the solar day. Since 1967, however, we have been blessed with an even more scientific definition: According to the *Bureau International des Poids et Mesures*, one second equals *the duration of 9,192,631,770 periods of the radiation corresponding to the transition between the two hyperfine levels of the ground state of the caesium 133 atom.* I kid you not.

It's tempting to put all our faith in Science, especially when it delivers such high falutin' definitions as the one above. Nevertheless, variations in the Earth's rotation continue to throw a monkey wrench into the clockworks, necessitating the occasional insertion of a "leap second." Please do not argue. You must just accept it. It's kind of like when your bank says you have 12 cents more/less in your account than your check register says you do. Don't do the math–life is short.

One casualty of our fancy new second is the familiar old standard, Greenwich Mean Time. GMT is now out of business. The new owner is UTC–Coordinated Universal Time. (I'm just letting you know so you can avoid an embarrassing *faux pas* at parties.)

Time sure has come a long way since it was measured with candles, incense sticks, sundials and obelisks, and the pendulum clock gave way to the pocket watch, which was replaced by the wrist watch, which no one under twenty-five wears anymore. UTC may have given us the automatic synchronization of every cell phone on the planet, but some of us pine for the theatricality of the hourglass, a graphic portrayal of the sands of time slowly eroding, down to the last grain. A cell phone, however, is a device that really should not be taken to the beach.

Even though Einstein laid it all out in his Special Theory of Relativity, there was still a large pocket of resistance insisting Time was an arrow going only in one direction. In 1969 the writer Kurt Vonnegut reminded us of other possibilities in his bestselling novel *Slaughterhouse Five*. The novel tells the story of Billy Pilgrim, who becomes un-stuck in Time and finds himself living pieces of his life all out of order. As Billy flits about the universe, he lands now and then on the planet of Tralfalmadore where the standard salutation is *Hello. Farewell.*

Some recent research has proposed that languages without verb tenses, such as Chinese, may endow their speakers with a larger, less confining sense of Time. Perhaps that gave them a leg up on the various predictions for Dec. 21, 2012, which belonged to one of two camps: the Doomsday Scenario, or the New Beginning. While it's certain that any doomsday–whether generic or prescription–would necessarily be followed by a new beginning, if we skipped the doomsday part I doubt if anyone would mind.

Shamans had another cognitive unit called the wheel of time... Time was like a tunnel of infinite length and width, a tunnel with reflective furrows. Every furrow was infinite, and there were infinite numbers of them. Living creatures were compulsorily made, by the force of life, to gaze into one furrow. To gaze into one furrow alone meant to be trapped by it, to live that furrow. A warrior's final aim is to focus, through an act of profound discipline, his unwavering attention on the wheel of time in order to make it turn. Warriors who have succeeded in turning the wheel of time can gaze into any furrow and draw from it whatever they desire. To be free from the spellbinding force of gazing into only one of those furrows means that warriors can look in either direction: as time retreats or as it advances on them.
–Carlos Castaneda, Introduction to *The Wheel of Time*, p. 8

The noted scholar Terence McKenna, who died in 2000 at the age of 53, said that his research had come up with the 12/21/2012 date independently of other indicators like solar flare activity or the Mayan Long Count Calendar. He was certain that this date would be a turning point for humanity. He may have been correct. Since scientists are still arguing about the nature of the

Universe, who's to say we DIDN'T slide into another dimension in December 2012?

Although it seems like not much happened, maybe we won't be so lucky next time. When will the next "2012" occur, and how should we prepare for it? Though sages far and wide have spoken at length on apocalyptic scenarios, the most apt advice may be from a drummer. My colleague, percussionist Eli Fountain, says simply, "Get a comfortable seat."

♪

ABOUT THE AUTHOR

Su Terry is a writer, composer, and saxophone and clarinet soloist.

Upon her arrival in New York in the early 1980s, Su was featured in bands led by Jazz Masters Charli Persip, Clifford Jordan, Walter Bishop, Jr. and Jaki Byard. She went on to play with greats such as Dr. Billy Taylor, Clark Terry, Al Jarreau, Chaka Khan, George Duke, Barry Harris, Hilton Ruiz, Irene Reid, Joe Lee Wilson, Teri Thornton, Tim Price, Mike Longo, Peggy Stern, Clarice Assad and Luiz Simas. She's been a jazz soloist with the National Symphony, the Brooklyn Philharmonic, the Hartford Symphony, the New York Pops and Florida Pops, and performs worldwide. Her discography currently contains over fifty recordings, including four as leader and three as co-leader.

Concurrently with her music career, Su worked professionally as a ghostwriter for scientific publications. She's the author of several music instruction books, three non-fiction books, and an illustrated short novel. She is a regular contributor to Allegro Magazine and lead columnist for The Note.

When she is not playing, writing or teaching, Su practices the martial art of taijiquan and is a USKSF Championship Tournament 8-time gold medalist.

More about her music career can be found in the books *Reed All About It* by Bob Bernotas, and *Madame Jazz* by Leslie Gourse.

Website: www.suterry.com
Twitter: http://twitter.com/SuTerryMusic

Su Terry is a Yamaha Saxophone Artist

www.ingramcontent.com/pod-product-compliance
Lightning Source LLC
Chambersburg PA
CBHW021337290326
41933CB00038B/829